P9-DUC-472

How to REALLY
Create a Successful
Marketing Plan

POINT LOMA NAZARENE UNIVERSITY
RYAN LIBRARY
3900 LOMALAND DRIVE
SAN DIEGO, CALIFORNIA 92106-2899

658.8
G974i3
4/99

Inc.
MAGAZINE
PRESENTS

HOW TO *Really* CREATE A

SUCCESSFUL MARKETING PLAN

■

BY DAVID E. GUMPERT

POINT LOMA NAZARENE UNIVERSITY
WITHDRAWN
RYAN LIBRARY

How to Really *Create a Successful Marketing Plan*
Copyright © 1996 Goldhirsh Group, Inc. All rights reserved. Printed in the United
States of America. No part of this book may be used or reproduced in any manner what-
soever without written permission except in the case of brief quotations embodied in
critical articles and reviews. For information, write:
Inc. Publishing, Attn: Permissions Manager,
38 Commercial Wharf, Boston, MA 02110–3883

Cover Design by S. Laird Jenkins Corporation
Text Design by Susan L. Dahl

This publication is designed to provide accurate and authoritative information
in regard to the subject matter covered. It is sold with the understanding that the
publisher is not engaged in rendering legal, accounting, or other professional service.
If legal advice or other expert assistance is required, the services of a competent
professional should be sought.

Library of Congress Card #96-77003

How to Really *Create a Successful Marketing Plan*
Includes Index
ISBN: 1-880394-25-1

Third edition

1   2   3   4   5   6   7   8   9   10

For my aunt, Inge Bleier,
who did so much to
encourage and inspire me.

ACKNOWLEDGMENTS

Because this is my third *Inc.* book, you'd think I'd have the process down pretty well by now. No such luck. This was the most challenging of the three, in large measure because marketing is such a complex subject. I was fortunate to have had the input of many thoughtful, knowledgeable people to help me overcome the many obstacles I encountered.

First and foremost, I must thank the entrepreneurs whose marketing plans and experiences are the basis of this book: Bob Bennett of MicroFridge, Jimmy Calano of CareerTrack, Tim DeMello of Wall Street Games, Ken Meyers of Smartfoods, Anita and Gordon Roddick of The Body Shop International, Marcy Syms of Syms, and Richard Worth of R.W. Frookies.

These entrepreneurs went beyond the normal bounds of sharing insights with a writer. They gave me amazing amounts of time and patiently explained their individual approaches to marketing. They also shared valuable data, documents, and ideas that helped make their companies successful—in the interest of making the market planning process easier for other executives.

A number of associates in their individual companies bent over backward to help me as well. They include David Bernard at Syms, Greg Davis at Wall Street Games, Steve Juedes at CareerTrack, and Scott McDermott at MicroFridge. I was also very fortunate to have had the input and guidance of a number of friends and associates during the months I spent on this book. Steve Snyder, chief operating officer of Software Partners/32 Inc. and a very skilled attorney, provided important counsel. David Boyd of Northeastern University, Bernie Tenenbaum of Fairleigh Dickenson University, Marty Marshall of Harvard Business School, Tom Melohn of North American Tool & Die, and Ruth Owades of Calyx & Corolla were kind enough to review the manuscript and provide useful suggestions.

Several *Inc.* Magazine staffers also went out of their way to provide suggestions for companies to include. Thanks to Nancy Lyons, Susan Greco, Leslie Brokaw, and Sara Baer-Sinnott.

While I get the credit as the author, others working behind the scenes made key contributions to the book. Jeanne Zimmermann provided essential editing touches, while Sue Dahl made the text accessible with her innovative page design.

The crew at *Inc.* provided its usual wonderful support. Special thanks to Hilary Glazer, Mary Ellen Mullaney, Jan Spiro, and Bob LaPointe.

And once again, my family bore the burden of my endless hours in front of the computer, and resulting irritability. Thanks to Jean, Laura, and Jason for your patience.

TABLE OF CONTENTS

Other business books from Inc. magazine

How to *Really* Start Your Own Business
- by David E. Gumpert

How to *Really* Create a Successful Business Plan
- by David E. Gumpert

How to *Really* Recruit, Motivate and Lead Your Team: Managing People
- Edited by Ruth G. Newman
  with Bradford W. Ketchum, Jr.

How to *Really* Deliver Superior Customer Service
- Edited by John R. Halbrooks

Anatomy of a Start-up: 27 Real-Life Case Studies
Why Some New Businesses Succeed and Others Fail
- Edited by Elizabeth K. Longsworth

301 Great Management Ideas From America's Most Innovative Small Companies
- Introduction by Tom Peters
- Edited by Sara P. Noble

Managing People: 101 Proven Ideas for Making You and Your People More Productive
from America's Smartest Small Companies
- Edited by Sara P. Noble

To receive a complete listing of *Inc.* Business books and videos, please call 1–800–468–0800 ext. 5435. Or write to *Inc.* Business Resources, P.O. Box 1365, Dept. 5435, Wilkes-Barre, PA 18703–1365.

How to REALLY Create a Successful Marketing Plan

YOUR MARKETING ADVENTURE

A Long and Winding Road

Marketing may be the single most important determinant of business success. Identifying prospects and figuring out how to turn them into customers is the essence of the business experience.

Yet marketing may also be the single most difficult aspect of business management. And it is becoming more difficult, because markets change faster and competition is more keen than ever. Techniques such as direct mail and advertising, which worked predictably a few years ago, don't necessarily work as expected anymore. Moreover, what works is constantly changing.

New competitors keep entering the marketplace as well. They can include franchises, major corporations, overseas companies, or your next-door neighbor who just lost his or her job. That is why planning has become more essential. Given the difficulties of marketing, the process of developing a marketing plan is really a trip down a long and winding road. It is a trip that everyone in business needs to take at one time or another. This book may be viewed as a road map designed to provide direction and sights to see along the way.

Just because it is difficult doesn't mean that developing a marketing plan is a bleak and unappealing experience. It is an adventure—a trip through the worlds of sociology, culture, psychology, technology, politics, quantitative analysis, and competition, among others.

This book draws on several resources to guide you:

• **The experiences of successful entrepreneurs.** One of the best ways to appreciate how to accomplish important business tasks is to observe how other successful entrepreneurs accomplished those tasks. In this book we draw on the experiences of seven companies.

I selected the companies with an eye toward diversity. They are in retailing, direct marketing, manufacturing, distribution, and services.

Some of the entrepreneurs shared their written plans with me, while some shared their recollections and important marketing documents that illustrate their approaches. The companies that shared their plans and recollections are:

• *The Body Shop International.* Founded in 1975 in England, this maker and retailer of cosmetics had grown to more than 1,000 stores worldwide by 1994. Founder Anita Roddick mixes natural products, politics, and information to attract a growing legion of loyal customers.

• *CareerTrack.* This Colorado company pioneered the $99 day-long self-improvement seminar when it was founded in 1982. It has become a specialist in using direct mail as a marketing tool, sending out millions of catalogs and other promotional pieces each year. Founder Jimmy Calano pushes the company constantly to refine and improve its marketing effectiveness.

• *R.W. Frookies.* This is a New York maker of the first mass-market healthful cookies. Within four years of its founding in 1987, it had grown to $15 million in annual sales. Founder Richard Worth is an authority on the food business.

• *MicroFridge.* This Massachusetts company distributes a combination microwave oven-refrigerator-freezer, primarily for use in college dormitories. After a slow start in 1987, the company grew to $12 million in sales by the mid-1990s.

• *Smartfoods.* One of the most successful snack food companies ever launched, Smartfoods and its Smartfood cheddar cheese popcorn grew to become the dominant precooked popcorn in the Northeast by the late 1980s, when it was acquired by Frito Lay.

• *Syms.* This pioneer in the off-price clothing retail business has grown from humble beginnings in Lower Manhattan in the late 1950s. By the mid-1990s, it had expanded nationally to nearly 40 stores.

• *Replica Corp.,* better known by its service line, Wall Street Games. By providing would-be stock market investors with pretend money and keeping tabs on how their stocks do, the company tapped into a whole new market. It also established alliances with such major players as AT&T and *USA Today.* By the early 1990s, it had expanded into the sports area.

• **My experiences in the marketing area.** Having covered marketing as an editor for the *Harvard Business Review*, I have had the opportunity to learn about the discipline from many of the best marketing experts in the country. In addition, I have read through dozens of marketing plans and assisted entrepreneurs in developing their plans. In that experience, I have developed my "road map" to creating successful marketing plans.

• **Exercises and advice.** Each chapter concludes with exercises designed to overcome common obstacles that come up in preparing and writing a marketing plan. These exercises represent coordinated steps that, when completed as suggested, result in a usable and highly focused marketing plan.

A Preview

Organizationally, this book is divided into three parts based on the broad tasks associated with developing a marketing plan:

1. The Task at Hand

Here I consider basic misconceptions and truths about marketing, personal characteristics necessary for successful marketing, and the nature of the marketing plan.

2. Devising a Strategy

This section assesses the major strategic issues that must be tackled. These include getting a handle on the market's size and complexities, along with your position in that market and an assessment of the competition.

3. Taking Action

This is the nitty-gritty of execution. Using the strategic issues, you develop an action plan with specific tasks and quantitative goals. The more detailed this action plan is, the more effective you will be in mobilizing the organization.

As difficult as it is, developing and writing a marketing plan is one of the most exciting and rewarding business tasks you will ever undertake. Hopefully, this book will add to both your excitement and rewards.

PART 1:

THE TASK
AT HAND

YOUR MARKETING PLAN

*Turning Art
into Science*

S imply stated, marketing is the process of identifying prospects and determining how best to turn them into customers. But there is nothing simple about marketing. It is at once fun and frustrating, obvious and elusive, conceptual and tactical.

In my view, it is bigger than many entrepreneurs realize. It requires a knowledge of history, sociology, culture, geography, and human nature, as well as competitive trends, positioning, and pricing. I can go on at length about its inherent contradictions and challenges, but probably the most useful analogy is to think of marketing as an art form.

Learning any art—painting, ballet, fiction writing, carpentry, or karate—

is invariably a lifelong process, with no guarantees of success. So it is with marketing. But as any art is broken down into its major components, made measurable, and regularly practiced, it becomes more easily mastered.

The more involved we become with a particular art form, the more we are able to get past the mysteries that awed us as outside observers. We become aware of a particular mind-set and of patterns that help make solutions more easily identifiable. Many of our reactions become automatic; for example, a black belt in karate reacts to a punch or a kick from an opponent nearly without thinking.

Just as courses in art, dance, writing, and woodworking can help bring out the talent we may have in that field, so can similar training in marketing. It is essential if one is going to write a marketing plan.

This book may be viewed as a short course in marketing, enabling you to write a marketing plan. It will help you move away from dealing with marketing solely on a gut level—as a mysterious art form—by breaking it down and allowing you opportunities to practice its various facets. I don't pretend to have the magical formula that transforms the art of marketing into a science, and I doubt that anyone does. But if this book is doing its job, it will move you in that direction.

Marketing Misconceptions: The Limits of Our Understanding

An important distinction between marketing and other art forms is that many entrepreneurs who may not believe themselves to be talented in such fields as art or carpentry, or even in more familiar business areas such as financing and accounting, think of themselves as experts in marketing. Much as in politics, individuals form opinions and viewpoints concerning marketing that they feel very strongly about—typically with insufficient information or expertise.

That's because we are constantly exposed to marketing approaches and strategies—when we walk through shopping malls, watch television commercials, stand in line at a bank, eat at a restaurant, or read direct-mail catalogs. Who among us doesn't have a view about how a clothing store's selection could have been made more attractive, how ads for food or beer turned us off, how a bank might speed up its lines, or how a restaurant could improve its service?

In these and dozens of other situations, we are reacting to some aspect of a company's marketing approach. Certainly having a view about someone else's business—even if it is based on insufficient or incorrect information—is fairly harmless.

The problem comes when you have strong views about your own business based on erroneous assumptions. Indeed, having misconceived views about your own business can be downright dangerous. You can quickly move down the wrong path and, before you have time to correct your mistakes, go out of business.

Obtaining the necessary information and coming to the correct conclusions about which marketing direction to take, however, is no easy task. It is the essence of moving marketing from the realm of art into that of science. Clearly, such a move isn't just desirable, it is essential.

To begin moving in the right direction, we must first dispose of some misconceptions that surround the subject of marketing. Four of the most common are:

This is a notion that is at once seductive and destructive. It likely stems from the fabulous success of mass manufacturers, beginning with Henry Ford and his Model T, to sell huge quantities of whatever they produced.	**Misconception 1: Companies control market demand.**

Indeed, if you look at the case of Smartfoods, it's easy to conclude at first glance that the company took control of demand for high-quality cheddar cheese popcorn. After all, there were no other similar products on the market when the founders started selling their unusual brand, Smartfood, in the distinctive black bag in 1984 and 1985. Its main direct competitors were producers of greasy orange-colored composition-cheese-and-popcorn snack foods.

If Ken Meyers and his partners had believed they controlled market demand for their product in 1985 and 1986, they might have tried to expand sales by raising investment or loan funds and pumping millions into mass-media advertising. But Meyers and his partners knew the company had to adapt to the much more powerful forces of the market. Among these forces were the movement by a growing number of consumers away from junk food and toward healthful food (hence the product name, Smartfood), tastier food, and companies they could feel good about.

Smartfoods' founders understood these forces. Thus, the company resisted the urge to do conventional advertising and instead concentrated on its unconventional "guerrilla marketing" approaches, which included such tactics as passing out free samples and sending specially decorated Smartfoods vans to events (like ski races and bicycle races) where its kind of consumers hung out.

At one point, recalls Meyers, he almost went the conventional advertising route. "In the spring of 1985, we set aside about $100,000 for sales and marketing expenses, and I decided to call the advertising agencies to do some advertising. So we invited a number of Boston-area agencies in to pitch the business. . . . They pretty much recommended four weeks of radio advertising in one market—Boston. They told us it would cost about $87,000, and that we could do whatever we wanted with the other $13,000. We realized this was silly, so we decided that conventional means were not the way to go."

Instead, says Meyers, the founders became creative. "We realized that our greatest marketing tools were the packages themselves. Our thinking was that we could use them as individual advertisements to various consumers. So we began passing out samples. I believe that over the next seven years, we gave out somewhere in excess of 15 million samples."

The most vivid testimony that no one company controls a market comes from the fact that many competitors spent huge amounts trying to imitate the company's product, with unimpressive results. Meyers estimates that by the late 1980s, more than two dozen competitors had sprung up. Yet Smartfoods' share of the precooked popcorn market in New England, which had been as high as 55% when it was the only player, eroded only to 44% by 1989, when the company was acquired by Frito Lay. "The reason we retained market share was that we had retained brand loyalty," claims Meyers. Based on his analysis, it can be argued that Smartfoods helped create a totally new food category that the company marketed so well that it seemed to control the market.

The idea that companies control markets has been disproven most vividly in the industry where the misconception first took hold—the automobile industry. General Motors saw its market share plummet during the 1980s, despite pouring millions of dollars into television, magazine, and other mass-market advertising. The decline of huge department stores (Macy's), airlines (Pan Am), and computer companies (Wang) is further evidence that companies don't control markets, no matter how large their advertising budgets.

Misconception 2: Once you develop a marketing approach that works for your company, you've mastered marketing.

This may be the most dangerous misconception, because it can mislead entrepreneurs who are enjoying business success. Just think about all the business executives who have ridden the crest of marketing success, only to crash not much later.

Victor Kiam, who became a celebrity during the 1980s speaking and writing about his marketing prowess with Remington, saw sales slip substantially in the early 1990s. Bill Millard launched one of the fastest-growing franchises in history with Computerland in 1980, but by the end of the decade it was a shell of its former self. Lee Iacocca was discussed at one point during the mid-1980s as a Presidential candidate because of his genius in turning around Chrysler, until Chrysler needed a new turnaround by the early 1990s.

Remember when Western Union was synonymous with time-sensitive business communications, and IBM synonymous with computers? Remember when Rod

Canion of Compaq Computer was being promoted as one of the great marketing geniuses of the century?

These examples aren't meant as slights to the individuals or companies noted. My purpose in citing them is to make the point that everything looks easy when it works. But it should be clear to anyone who follows the ups and downs of business that few executives can feel truly secure that they have mastered marketing.

The converse of this is that a single overall explanation exists as to why successful marketers stumble. Successful marketers invariably attribute their accomplishments to some special practice—a focus on product quality or top-notch service or speedy delivery or the best prices. The stumbles come about, they typically say in retrospect, either because of some force beyond their control (Japanese imports or a recession, for example) or because they "took their eye off the ball."

If one analytically picks apart the successes and failures, though, they are invariably much more complicated. Lee Iacocca can certainly blame Japanese imports and a recessionary environment for Chrysler's problems in the early 1980s and again in the early 1990s. But there are no doubt a variety of pricing, feature, positioning, segmenting, promotional, and other issues that adversely affected the company. And perhaps Iacocca became more infatuated with his own success than he should have been if he were to stay objective about his company's marketing prospects.

Misconception 3: There's a magical "marketing bullet" that works for everyone.

15

Misconception 4: Marketing and selling are the same.

This misconception comes about because many of the most successful entrepreneurs are also very good salespeople. Talented salespeople can often go a long way selling a particular product or service without having a clear understanding of the true dynamics of the marketplace. Thus their success in selling can delude them into believing they have mastered marketing.

In reality, though, selling is only one aspect of marketing implementation. That is, once you have identified your customer prospects and determined how best to reach them, you move into the sales process—convincing customers to buy your product or service. If you haven't done your marketing homework, you can easily fail when it comes to selling. And if you are fortunate enough to convince a random group of individuals or companies to buy your product or service, without some notion as to why you picked them, your success may be a testimonial to your sales rather than your marketing skills.

Bob Bennett of MicroFridge may have stumbled early on because of such confusion. When Bennett commissioned independent distributors who specialize in selling to appliance stores, he ran into trouble. "It was almost like a sales prevention program. These are people who sell to appliance stores. . . . They are order takers." He subsequently dispensed with that approach and came to some important realizations about the real marketing issues confronting MicroFridge, which are discussed later in this chapter.

This confusion between marketing and sales often

becomes apparent when companies seek to move past a particular sales plateau—typically in the $500,000 to $3-million range. For example, an East Coast consulting company that specializes in assisting company reorganizations was stuck for three years during the mid-1980s at about $1.5 million annual sales, after more than ten years in business. A marketing-oriented chief executive was finally recruited and determined that the problem was the company's erratic approach to marketing. The company's founder was a great salesperson who would sell a few substantial contracts, recruit a team to do the work, and then dive in to complete the contracts. After the contracts were completed and business threatened to flounder, the founder would go out and look for some new customers, and sell them. Unfortunately, he gave little attention to consistency either in identifying target markets or in developing a marketing theme. The new CEO corrected the problems and, as of the early 1990s, the company was nearing $10 million in annual sales and growing at 30% annually.

Marketing Truths:
Moving Toward a More Rational Approach

Now that I have dispelled these marketing misconceptions, we can begin to examine some marketing truths. I have had the good fortune of being able to examine closely the marketing strategies and plans of seven very successful businesses: CareerTrack, R.W. Frookies, Syms, The Body Shop, Smartfoods,

Wall Street Games (Replica), and MicroFridge. They have helped me reach some important conclusions about the overall marketing experience that are essential to keep in mind as one goes through the process of developing a marketing plan.

• **True understanding of any market is more difficult than most entrepreneurs imagine.**

One theme that stands out about the companies I examined is that most stumbled badly at some point before their more visible success. Two years after starting up, Smartfoods was out of money and on the verge of going out of business. Similarly, MicroFridge found itself on the precipice with a warehouse full of its combination microwave ovens-refrigerators-freezers—and few buyers—after two years in business. Wall Street Games dragged for two years trying to sell its concept of stock market investing as a game before suddenly moving toward stardom.

In each of these cases, along with dozens of others that appear regularly in *Inc.* Magazine company profiles, the founders struggle to comprehend their markets. Often they head in the wrong direction for a surprisingly long time before they understand the error of their ways.

That isn't to say that some entrepreneurs don't hit pay dirt very quickly. That was the situation with R.W. Frookies and its healthful cookies, The Body Shop and its socially conscious cosmetic stores, and CareerTrack with its low-priced seminars. Unfortunately, these and other exceptions to the rule get the bulk of the business press's attention, leading to the unrealistic conclusion that coming up with a winning marketing formula is within the grasp of most people.

What seems "obvious" is in many cases just plain wrong. For instance, imagine that you are Bob Bennett in 1987 trying to get MicroFridge off the ground. Your market is administrators of college dormitories. Some of the administrators allow microwave ovens in the dorms and some prohibit them for fear of electrical overload, fires, insect infestations, or other reasons. Wouldn't you assume that the administrators most likely to want MicroFridge's appliance would be those that allowed them in the dorms?

Then you would have been wrong. Only after more dead ends than he cares to remember did Bennett determine that his company's best prospects were those who resisted allowing students to have microwave ovens. In those situations, he could demonstrate his company's benefits—students really wanted the appliances, they wouldn't create electrical problems and, most important, if students got their way, they were less likely to move out of the dorms. More students staying in the dorms meant fewer empty rooms and more income to the colleges, during a time of rising concern about filling college-owned dorms. With that realization, Micro-Fridge could concentrate its marketing energy on the best prospects, and sales soared.

Jimmy Calano similarly discovered a counterintuitive approach to successfully staying ahead of competitors in the dog-eat-dog world of self-improvement seminars. In 1982, when other seminar firms were charging $150 to $200 for day-long seminars, Calano pioneered the $99 seminar. By 1985, when his competitors had matched his price, he

• **The right marketing formula is often counterintuitive.**

shocked them again, by going to $45. While they scratched their heads wondering how he could ever make money at that price, Calano smiled to himself. "We knew that we would increase revenues substantially from sales of our self-help audio- and videotapes that we offer at all seminars as well as through our promotional catalogs," he says.

• Successful marketers solve problems.

If your product or service has achieved any level of success, it almost certainly solves a problem. Understanding the exact nature of the problem being solved is often the key to moving from modest success to great success. When Bob Bennett realized that his company was really solving a problem for dormitory administrators in helping hold students in the dorms, he made major progress. When Sy Syms came to the realization that he was not just providing off-price merchandise, but actually helping customers receive special value when they bought brand names at sizable savings, he similarly took an important step.

• The little things make a huge difference.

Back in 1990, a Toyota salesman demonstrating a Camry's features to me pulled the plastic coffee-cup holder out of the center of the front dashboard. "Believe it or not, this little thing has sold more cars for me than any other single feature," he said. He wasn't giving me a sales pitch, just making an observation. And indeed, when I brought my wife in to see the car, the coffee-cup holder was what sold her on a car she initially believed was too expensive.

In marketing, the details are often key to success. Tim

DeMello, founder of Wall Street Games, has discovered that the details of his marketing implementation plan—such items as the mailing dates of direct-mail advertisements and the time television commercials run—have a huge impact on the bottom line. If TV commercials stimulate more calls from potential participants in the company's investment and sports contests than expected, then the telephone banks will be undermanned and many calls will go unanswered. Not only will sales opportunities be lost, but potential customers will be turned off by their difficulty in getting through to the company.

Similarly, Jimmy Calano has focused CareerTrack on such small details as making sure all telephone inquiries are answered on the second ring and nearly all questions are answered by the first person to pick up the phone, so prospects don't have to endure annoying telephone transfers.

The decisions people make about whether to buy particular products or services are often emotional in nature. Companies that succeed invariably help people feel good about some basic emotional issue—hope, fear, guilt, or greed, for instance—better than competitors.

A fruit juice cookie of the type marketed by R.W. Frookies clearly plays on the guilt many people feel when they eat conventional sweets, laden with processed sugar. It also plays on their fears of heart disease, diabetes, and other health problems associated with eating no-no foods like cookies.

CareerTrack's seminars offer the hope of career ad-

• **Marketing success requires a keen understanding of human nature.**

vancement via gaining the right skills and knowledge. There's also an element of greed mixed in; making good use of the seminars can lead participants to achieve a significant financial return on their small investment of money and time, and possibly even great riches.

The Body Shop chain is probably the master manipulator of human emotions, although founder Anita Roddick doesn't like to view her company's success in such basic and, to her, crass terms. But clearly the company's opposition to animal testing of cosmetics, its advocacy of recycling, and its support of Third World economic-development efforts appeal to many consumers. They can indulge themselves in the company's not inexpensive cosmetics with the knowledge that some of their money is simultaneously helping three worthwhile causes: animals, the environment, and the Third World poor.

• Successful marketing strategies of similar companies may be quite different.

As noted earlier, there's no single magic marketing bullet that works for all companies. This observation can even be applied to companies with similar distribution systems or in the same industry. Syms and The Body Shop are both high-powered retailers of consumer goods, but their marketing strategies are diametrically opposed in key ways.

Syms's marketing strategy relies very heavily on the homespun, information-oriented television commercials featuring the company's founder, Sy Syms, telling viewers that, "An educated consumer is our best customer."

The Body Shop has long, and proudly, resisted the

advertising that is a given in the cosmetics business. "Just before we opened our first shop in the United States, *The Wall Street Journal* ran an article quoting a Harvard Business School professor saying that we would require a major advertising campaign," recalls Anita Roddick. "I put that quote on a postcard that we distributed to our shops, with my response: 'I'll never hire anybody from Harvard Business School.' " Instead, the company relies on a combination of the simple attractiveness of its shops and the extensive free publicity it receives from newspaper and magazine write-ups on its unusual philosophy of being a good corporate citizen.

The days when a company could count on revving up demand for its products or services by simply throwing huge amounts of money into advertising are over. Even in the seemingly different approaches of Syms and The Body Shop, there is an important similarity: Both companies rely on old-fashioned "word of mouth" to bring customers in.

• Unconventional marketing strategies are becoming increasingly acceptable.

Marcy Syms, the company's president and the daughter of founder Sy Syms, points out that the company never advertises its popular twice-yearly sales. The huge crowds that descend on Syms around the country go there based entirely on word of mouth. "With each event, the crowds get bigger," she notes. "It happens with each new store we open." Similarly, Anita Roddick credits The Body Shop's fast-growing popularity in Europe and the United States in significant measure to word of mouth.

Increasing numbers of successful entrepreneurs are extolling a marketing approach popularly known as guerrilla marketing. Basically, it involves the use of unconventional, low-cost tactics to gain attention. As noted earlier, Ken Meyers attributes the amazing success of Smartfood cheddar cheese popcorn to such tactics, which included using a bag different in appearance from other snack foods, passing out free product samples at bicycle races and marathons, dressing skiers up in human-size bags, and flying promotional banners from planes.

Underlying such unconventional approaches are two basic premises: distinguishing one company's product or service from competitors and getting maximum value from each marketing dollar. The competition in nearly every market is so intense and the costs associated with entering the marketplace potentially so high that unconventional marketing approaches can be expected to gain increasing amounts of attention in the future.

• Successful marketers understand the buyer's perspective.

It is essential for entrepreneurs to be able to view their companies and the products and services they offer from the viewpoint of prospective customers. This is never easy, nor can it be completely achieved because of the emotional involvement owners inevitably have with their customers, but it is an important goal to strive for. The effective use of information, relief of guilt, problem solving, and other techniques by the entrepreneurs profiled in this book are testimony to their ability to keep the customer's viewpoint consistently uppermost.

Beginning Your Marketing Plan

What does all this have to do with writing a marketing plan? Quite a lot.

For one thing, moving from art to science implies becoming quantitative and precise. Researchers keep track of how much of each chemical goes into a test tube or how much medication at what frequency was injected into a lab mouse, and then write down the results, with an eye toward quantifiable and consistent data. They compare results over time. There will be more about the quantitative issues in subsequent chapters.

For another thing, applying some of the observations made here to your own situation is most effectively done in writing. I have provided exercises at the end of this chapter to ease that process. As anyone who has ever tried to write a business plan is well aware, the hardest part of the writing process is getting started. Applying the observations here via the exercises enables you to get past this most serious of all planning obstacles. When you are finished with this chapter, you will have actually begun to write your plan.

► **Exercises**

1. Are any marketing misconceptions at work in your company? If so, describe them and provide suggestions for overcoming them.

2. Describe at least one driving force in your market that is counterintuitive.

3. Describe at least one problem that your company solves for prospective customers.

4. Develop and describe at least two unconventional marketing approaches you should consider for your company's products or services.

5. List and describe at least two emotional forces at work that determine success in your market.

6. List and describe at least three seemingly minor implementation tasks, or details, that must be dealt with to succeed in your market.

(Worksheets for this chapter are provided on page 269)

THE MARKETING OVERVIEW

Your View of the World

It should be evident that successful marketing requires a wide variety of skills and talents. Few people have them all.

But the way you assess your market and write your plan is as much a function of how you view the world and your company's role in it as anything else. Are you a creative genius à la Anita Roddick of The Body Shop or a detail-oriented implementer such as Marcy Syms of Syms clothing stores or Tim DeMello of Wall Street Games?

The previous chapter should have provided some insights as to things your company is doing right from a marketing perspective and where it might need to fill in gaps. It should also have gotten you thinking about your company's marketing mission: its overall role and goals in the marketplace.

In this chapter, I focus on creating an initial draft of a written overview of your company's marketing approach. The purpose is to ease you into the particulars of the plan and keep you in a writing mode. That way, when I offer an approach in Chapter 3 for structuring the marketing plan, you will discover you have already considered certain aspects of it.

Your Marketing Personality

In my experiences with entrepreneurs, I have come to the conclusion that each has what might be called a marketing personality, which is an extension of that person's everyday personality.

It determines how you view not only the world at large but your company's role in that world. This matter of worldly views and how you deal with them isn't just of idle intellectual curiosity. As I pointed out at the beginning of the first chapter, marketing encompasses your assessment of historical trends, international and domestic politics, and human values.

An important first step is to determine what your personal marketing strengths and weaknesses are. Then it's possible not only to build on your strengths but to compensate for your weaknesses by getting additional training, adding appropriate people with the needed skills, or locating the right consultants who have the tools you are missing.

To help in assessing your marketing personality, I have developed a number of criteria that I believe are essential for marketing success. They are:

The ability to envision a new enterprise and how it will be marketed—especially one that hasn't been tried before—is a special talent. Certainly Steve Jobs and Stephen Wozniak must be credited with vision in starting Apple Computer in 1977. Computers were not a new item when they started the company, but they correctly saw that the wide availability of semiconductor chips made possible a whole new industry—computers for personal use.

• Vision.

Ted Turner's creation of Cable News Network can be placed in the same category. He saw the new communication opportunities being opened by cable television and satellites and coupled those trends with the human desire for ever more immediate news about the world.

Even a novice businessperson can't help but be impressed by the creativity evident in a Body Shop store or on a Smartfood bag. Just a brief conversation with Anita Roddick, founder of The Body Shop, is enough to get a listener's head spinning as she pours out creative idea after idea. Among them: sell cosmetics off of trucks in Rumania, provide audio tours of stores, use stores for voter registration, inaugurate a Native American project, and on and on. She is adamant that other Body Shop executives avoid conventional business thinking; indeed, The Body Shop purposely doesn't even have a marketing department, but a Department of Damn Good Ideas. "It's me and a few other people," she says. "I set priorities and we set dates by which things have to be done."

• Creativity.

Creativity should be distinguished from vision, however. While there's no indication that Anita Roddick had a vision of the huge chain of stores that the Body Shops have become, she had the creativity to provide the right choreography that is an essential component of each Body Shop store.

• Sense of timing.

Being the first with the most isn't necessarily a guarantee of marketing success. Just ask entrepreneurs who started businesses in the 1970s and 1980s to provide telephone grocery-delivery services, superconductor products, and solar energy products, among others. It's not that their service or product concepts were bad or wrong. They were just too early. The market wasn't quite ready for them.

Had Richard Worth tried to start R.W. Frookies in the 1970s, he may well have failed because he might have been marketing a product that not enough consumers were ready to accept. He explains how he succeeded in the 1980s by observing in marketing-speak: "We had a specific marketing plan, but the timing was very important. When you have a what and a when, you have something. The whats and the whens interact. Timing is an awesome part of marketing."

Similarly, Bob Bennett might have been too early with his combination microwave ovens-refrigerators-freezers had he put them out in the early 1980s, when the appliance was less common and college dormitory administrators were less worried about keeping dorms occupied than they were in the late 1980s and 1990s.

The trends that made possible the success of Smartfoods, R.W. Frookies, and others in this book were evident to many of us on some level. But only a few individuals correctly digested the social, cultural, political, and other trends in such a way as to come up with the products or services that worked.

• Ability to spot key trends.

These entrepreneurs clearly have more than an ability to spot trends. They have an ability to see through the smoke and noise that typically obscure fundamental changes—the desire for guilt-free snacks among a growing number of consumers, for example—to put together a plan that makes success possible.

As noted previously, successful marketing is dependent on an ability to anticipate and tend to details that might escape other people. These details, like answering the phone on the second ring, go a long way toward making an ordinary concept like low-cost self-improvement seminars a smashing success. Alternately, a great concept can be rendered useless by an inability to execute the details.

• Penchant for details.

Unfortunately, the great visionaries or creative thinkers of marketing fame are often unable to cope with the details that make their concepts succeed. Anita Roddick, who is clearly not a detail person, has been very fortunate to have her husband, Gordon, oversee much of The Body Shop's marketing implementation.

Ultimately, every company's marketing strategy is shaped by its customers, and they are constantly changing.

• Ability to change.

Indeed, they are changing more quickly than ever in their tastes, desires, and needs. Entrepreneurs must be willing and able to see important changes in their markets and then lead their companies to make necessary adjustments. Companies that succeed early on often seem to have difficulty dealing with subsequent change. Either they fail to see the changes or, if they do see them, they misunderstand their implications. Minicomputer companies, department stores, and major airlines are just a few of the types of companies that stumbled badly in the late 1980s and early 1990s because of their failure to deal properly with change.

• A long-term viewpoint.

Successful selling is typically concerned with short-term, here-and-now, what-have-you-done-for-me-lately kind of thinking. Successful marketing requires being able to look ahead three to five years. That distinction helps explain why a completely sales-oriented personality often has difficulty putting together a marketing plan. Effective market planning sometimes even requires passing up sales opportunities, as well as considering issues beyond sales (economic and political changes, technological improvements, and other matters).

• Focus.

Entrepreneurs are often tempted to go after more markets than they should. This tendency is typically the result of trying to produce and sell too many products or services. Because it is so difficult to understand a single market well, trying to understand several well enough to succeed is often impossible.

Highly focused entrepreneurs tend to go after markets

sequentially. Bob Bennett thus focused MicroFridge's initial attention on college dormitories. Once he had successfully penetrated that market, he turned his attention to the hotel and motel market. Similarly, Tim DeMello initially concentrated on attracting individuals interested in Wall Street Games' simulated stock market game. Only after he was well established in that area did he move on to sports enthusiasts interested in picking winning sports teams.

How strongly do you feel about the benefits of your company's product or service? More important, how is your passion relayed to prospective customers? You don't have to listen very long to Anita Roddick to realize she is very

• **Passion.**

Writing Tips

As you think about your company's market, write down your observations, with the following in mind:

• Use the approach that is most comfortable for you. For some executives, the best approach is to write in traditional prose. For others, terse lists serve better. And for those who are visually oriented, diagrams or drawings may do the best job.

• Write in brief spurts. Avoid getting hung up trying to capture everything in a single sitting. Capture one idea as you are inspired, and then write some more another time.

• Rewrite extensively. Let your plan sit for a day or two after each writing effort and then come back to it to restate or reorganize your thoughts. That process invariably improves the writing over time.

passionate about The Body Shop and what it stands for. Her passion comes through in the company's newsletters, brochures, videotapes, and store displays.

A sense of passion can sometimes make up for other deficiencies. Prospective customers will often give the benefit of the doubt to a product or service if they sense a passionate commitment from the company's executives.

• A technology and information orientation.

Successful marketing increasingly depends on an entrepreneur's ability to make effective use of marketing data and information, typically through use of computers. Both Jimmy Calano of CareerTrack and Tim DeMello of Wall Street Games credit their success to their adroit use of databases to market their products and services. They maintain vast lists of prospective customers and monitor responses to mailings. DeMello has also expended much effort and expense to keep tabs of the investment choices participants make, much like a brokerage firm.

Anita Roddick also owes much of The Body Shop's success to her early realization that consumers are interested in as much information as possible about the cosmetics products they purchase—where the ingredients originate, what effect they have on the skin or hair, and how to maximize a product's effectiveness. The company includes that kind of information on shelf placards and in the plentiful brochures available in stores.

Capturing the Essentials: An Overview

What is your company's and your personal approach to marketing success? As you begin putting together a marketing plan, you should think about this basic question and capture your answer in writing. The form is much less important than the simple fact of doing the writing.

One useful technique is to summarize your company's approach in a half page to a page of prose. As you do that, consider the issues raised in these two chapters. Incorporate the answers you wrote down in the exercise at the end of Chapter 1. Have you allowed for the fact that markets drive companies? Are you describing an approach to marketing or an approach to selling? If you have achieved marketplace success, can you think of ways to improve on that success? Have you considered how the market might be changing? Are you giving thought to unconventional approaches? Are you aware of counterintuitive factors at work?

Think also about your personal attributes. What sparks of creativity have you added to your marketing approach that sets it apart from conventional approaches in your industry? How appropriate is your sense of timing, given changes going on in your industry? What fundamental social, economic, cultural, or other trends does your marketing approach take advantage of?

To give you two models of how you might approach this matter, I have excerpted from overview planning statements of two companies: CareerTrack and MicroFridge (see Exhibits 2–1 and 2–2 on pages 39–40). They do a good job of focusing on the main ideas, or big picture.

CareerTrack's statement from its 1990 plan begins by explaining the company's position in its market—that it has achieved dominance in an industry comprised of very small firms. More important, the company describes what sets it apart from competitors and lists the factors it believes will enable it to maintain leadership, such as low price, creative approaches to direct mail, and speakers known to satisfy audiences. The list of items at the end relate to the details of marketing implementation success—a focus on customer service and much in-house attention to developing new seminar topics. The company conveys a great deal about its marketing approach in a single paragraph.

MicroFridge's terse list essentially describes its primary customer prospects and the most compelling reasons for them to buy from the company. Bob Bennett points out that MicroFridge has only begun to penetrate a market that has vast potential. He concentrates on issues of importance to prospective buyers: the dorms need to keep students and the students place a premium on convenience. In addition, he notes a key detail: wiring is a constraint for conventional microwaves and their large draw on electrical power in many dorms, which gives an advantage to the company's patented electrical system that doesn't strain conventional wiring. There are no wasted words—just the driving forces that Bennett identified as the ones he and his company's executives should always keep in mind as they plan their strategy and implementation.

The Case Method Approach to Beginning a Plan

A teaching method made popular by the Harvard Business School is the case method approach. Students at Harvard spend most of their time reading and discussing company case histories ranging from 2 pages to 35 or 40 pages. These are essentially narratives about the histories, people, and decision making within small and large companies alike. Such companies as Federal Express, L.L. Bean, Hartmann Luggage, and Levi Strauss are the subjects of HBS cases. Some cases relate most directly to marketing, others to finance, and still others to organizational management.

At first glance, many of the marketing cases are leisurely written discourses on how the company was founded, what its initial marketing approach was, how the market changed, how executives reacted to the changes, and what decisions the company faced at the time the case was written.

Professors then pose questions about the cases that relate to issues being taught. They ask students whether the company's strategy is appropriate or whether major changes are in order. Students must support their position based on the facts in the case.

Writing a case about your own company is an excellent technique for getting started on a marketing plan, according to Marty Marshall, a professor of marketing at the Harvard Business School and longtime director of its Owners/Presidents Management Program. In notes he distributes to business owners, he suggests, "In writing up 'your story or case:'

"How did your business get started? When? Why? Typically, most of you begin by saying that you or someone else saw a problem and proceeded to solve it.

"What is the evolution of your business since its inception? Usually this part of the story begins to get into the details of the industry, of the market, and of the strategy of the business.

"The story then goes on over into the principal parts of a marketing plan."

Approaches for organizing the marketing plan are the subject of the next chapter.

▶ ## Exercises

1. **Assessing Your Marketing Personality**
   Here is a list of the key components of the marketing personality. Rate yourself on a scale of 1 to 5 (with 5 being the strongest) in each category. A score of 3 or lower in any one category suggests you need assistance in that category.

Category	Rating (1–5)
Vision	
Creativity	
Sense of timing	
Ability to spot key trends	
Penchant for details	
Ability to change	
A long-term viewpoint	
Passion	
Focus	
A technology and information orientation	

2. Preparing a Marketing Overview

a. Write a "case" about your company and the evolution of its marketing approach.

b. Use this case to prepare a half-page to one-page marketing overview that describes your company's approach for achieving marketing success.

(Worksheets for this chapter are provided on page 272)

FROM THE MARKETING PLAN OF ★ CAREERTRACK ★

EXHIBIT 2–1

CAREERTRACK: CONTINUED MARKET LEADERSHIP

(1990 Plan)

CareerTrack has a strong market position in the highly fragmented seminar industry. Although thousands of small consulting firms conduct seminars of one type or another, there are only a handful of seminar companies with annual sales greater than $20 million. The two firms with revenues greater than the Company's typically concentrate on high-cost, multi-day seminars. The Company believes that relative to the few firms with substantial activity in the single-day seminar business, it has numerous competitive advantages, including lower registration fees, a uniquely successful system of selling publications at the seminars, higher-quality speakers, exceptional customer service, aggressive new seminar development, in-house media buying, innovative direct-marketing strategies, and the Company's line of exclusive designer-line seminars.

EXHIBIT 2-2

FROM THE MARKETING PLAN OF
MICROFRIDGE

MICROFRIDGE:
BUSINESS OVERVIEW BY MARKET

The College and University Market

Market Overview:
- Approximately 1.25 million rooms with no major growth.
- MFI share is approximately 0.7% of rooms.
- Enrollments and occupancies declining.
- Retention becoming major goal.
- Convenience is major selling point of dormitory living.
- Price for room and board is important.
- Wiring is constrained.
- Conservative buyers, herd mentality.
- 43% of universities allow microwaves.
- MFI has 200+ units per active college program.

THE BEST PLAN FOR YOU

*Assessing
the Options*

What is a marketing plan? How does it differ from a business plan? Are there variations of marketing plans for different stages and types of businesses? What subjects should a marketing plan address?

These are among the questions likely to occur to you as you prepare a plan. But before addressing these questions, another more fundamental and pressing one should be considered: Why write a marketing plan at all? For unless you are convinced you need a plan, you either won't do it or you'll fail to to do it well enough to gain all its benefits.

In light of the two previous chapters, the answer should be fairly evident by this time. Indeed, I intentionally placed this chapter here to make the question easy to answer. A textbook explanation at the start of the book about the importance of a written plan, and of how global and wide-ranging a subject marketing is, likely wouldn't count for much. A more meaningful approach is to get a taste, through a few of the experiences of the successful featured entrepreneurs, of just how complex and essential marketing and the associated planning really are.

Moreover, I have noted several times how the pace of marketplace change, always rapid, seems to be accelerating. We all know from reading the business press that the volume of market-related data and the rapidity of competitors appearing and disappearing has increased.

While all this seems to be an effective argument for formal planning, a logical question can be raised: How can one write a plan if the marketplace is so complex and is changing so rapidly? More to the point, why should one write a plan under those circumstances?

Actually, it is because the marketplace is so complex and changing so quickly that planning has become more essential. Everyone has a plan in his or her head. But it is only when it gets written down that inconsistencies, unknowns, gaps, and implausibilities become identified and can be dealt with.

A well-conceived written plan serves several other important purposes as well:

• **It gives you an anchor.** In a fast-changing business climate, any stability is welcome. With a written marketing plan, you have something to go back to for measuring your progress. You also have the ability to incorporate changes as you learn more about your market and as your goals shift over time.

• **It forces you to look ahead.** An executive's natural tendency is to consider the recent past and simply project that into the future. But with markets changing as quickly as they are, a forward-looking approach is imperative.

• **It helps focus the management team on key marketing issues.** Without the framework provided by a plan, managers are inclined to focus on day-to-day affairs and lose sight of the big picture. With a plan, everyone is working toward the same goals and understands how to implement them.

• **It leads to an implementation timetable.** This helps assure that executives don't gradually drift away from the plan's overall goals. When they know that certain tasks and goals are to be completed by certain times, the executives tend to remain focused on the key marketing issues.

It is important to make a related point to help ease anxieties you might be feeling about the prospect of writing a plan: The best plan for you is the one that best meets your company's short-term and long-term needs. As you'll see in the remainder of this chapter, you have a great deal of flexibility in determining how to organize and write your plan. One type of plan does not fit all companies.

What Is a Marketing Plan?

A marketing plan is an unusual beast in the business world. There isn't a single accepted model that one can follow as there is with a business plan. Nor has a lot been written about marketing plans. Yet over the years, increasing numbers of executives have felt the need to prepare marketing plans for their companies. (I explore the individual approaches of several companies later in this chapter.)

A marketing plan is as much a process as a document that guides your company in accomplishing three essential tasks:

1. Identifying the key marketing issues that determine your company's long-term success.

This is a combined research, analytical, and creative process, leading to development of a strategy. You assess what's going on in the marketplace as it affects your company and make decisions about which groups of prospects offer the best opportunities.

This part of the process is typically led by the chief executive. At MicroFridge, Bob Bennett as founder and chief executive has had responsibility for identifying the key marketing issues facing the company. "This company was formed to leverage my sales and marketing skills," he says. "It could be shoes or refrigerators. I like to sell. The reason we survived is that I was able to sell Penn State or Boston University on buying our product. I was also able to sell private investors and venture capitalists on investing. It's basically been a sales game based on a workable marketing strategy."

2. Mobilizing your organization around the same marketing-related tasks and goals.

Once you have developed your strategy, you need to determine who in your company will do what so the strategy is implemented. Who will have responsibility for developing a marketing budget, monitoring expenses, overseeing the sales process, and putting together a promotion program? As Bennett notes, once his company had achieved its first profits, in 1991, "The real challenge became to disseminate my ideas and goals to the troops." That way, everyone will be working toward the same goals.

At Wall Street Games, some employees help write the plan and actually sign it. The effect is to involve and commit them by assigning them direct responsibility for whether or not it works.

The best marketing plans are those that are not only based on past accomplishments but also provide specific ways to measure success. Key to doing that is determining which data should be collected. In direct mail, key data involves recipient response rates, broken down as specifically as possible according to location, income, and mailing list source, for example. Effective measurement lays the groundwork for future plans.

Budgeting is also important because it represents the most serious kind of commitment a company can make to a plan. It is one thing to come up with strategies and another to get people organized around those strategies. But once a company begins apportioning its financial resources, it will need to measure the return on those resources.

At CareerTrack, budgeting takes place over a period of weeks as employees discuss how to turn the marketing plan's goals and tactics into actual quantities of catalogs to be printed, the mix of seminar topics, and the titles and quantities of video- and audiotapes to offer for sale.

According to Steve Juedes, director of marketing at CareerTrack, a major part of the budgeting process is to review the results of the previous year's budget. Which items worked as expected in bringing in business and which didn't? What ideas do people have for new approaches and products? To ensure there aren't any big surprises, he notes, fol-

3. Measuring your company's effectiveness in identifying and attracting customers.

The Best Plan for You

3

low-up meetings are held quarterly to determine how projections are measuring up to budget. "We are constantly reviewing and questioning our assumptions, and looking for evidence to support or contradict them," he says.

A Marketing Plan vs. A Business Plan

A fair amount of confusion exists between marketing plans and business plans. Mention a marketing plan to some executives and they think you mean a business plan. For other executives, the reverse is true.

The reason for the confusion is that the terms are often used interchangeably. But it is also because executives hear what they need to hear. If your primary concern is with the marketing function of your business, then when someone talks about how you should put together a business plan, you may well be thinking "marketing plan" as you nod in agreement. The distinctions are only important insofar as they affect your particular situation, however.

Here are some comparisons between marketing and business plans that may help explain the matter:

• Selling vs. guiding.

Business plans are meant to sell a company to stakeholders, such as financial backers, key executives, and even the owners. Marketing plans are designed to guide companies along a particular path. The reason for the difference stems from the way business and marketing plans have traditionally been used. Business plans are frequently used to raise investment and loan funds. Marketing plans are used primarily as internal planning documents.

Because business plans are typically prepared for outside consumption and marketing plans for internal use, marketing plans are more informal than business plans. The business plan is typically broken down into five to seven sections with similar titles, no matter what the stage of business or the industry (i.e., The Company, Markets, Products/Services, Finance). As you'll see later in this chapter, marketing plans can be broken down in any of several ways to best fit your needs.

• **Degree of formality.**

3

The Best Plan for You

Who Should Write the Plan?

This question comes up with regard to any company-wide plan. The answer depends on what works best for your particular situation:

• The CEO writes the plan. He or she then circulates a draft to other members of the management team, who provide their ideas and inputs.

• Each of several executives researches and writes a section of the plan. The sections are typically divided according to their areas of responsibility. Then the sections are reviewed by all concerned managers, and the ideas and issues debated and made consistent.

• The plan is written committee style. This takes place over a period of several weeks, usually during lengthy meetings. Using this approach, though, one person invariably assumes responsibility for turning the consensus view into a written form.

Whichever approach you choose, be sure to establish a schedule, with strict deadlines, for completing such tasks as an outline, an initial draft, and rewrites.

With the previous two points in mind, it should also be noted that it sometimes isn't clear whether a particular plan is a marketing plan or a business plan. In some cases, the marketing plan is simply a chapter in the business plan. But sometimes marketing is such a major component of the business plan that it is difficult to determine what kind of a plan one is really dealing with.

Three of the five written marketing plans I examined for this book are really sections of business plans, albeit large parts. In the case of MicroFridge, the marketing plan is a section of a business plan intended to guide company management, with the marketing section comprising 18 of 22 written pages. CareerTrack's 1990 plan was intended to raise investment funds for the company, but 17 of 27 pages are given over to marketing. (The 1991 plan, which is excerpted later in the book, similarly emphasizes marketing.)

Terminology isn't really the key issue. Call it a business plan or a marketing plan, but either way you must deal completely with the marketing issues that are most pressing for your company now and in the future. The marketing issues are nearly always the ones that determine success in other business areas like finance and manufacturing.

I refer to a marketing plan to describe a plan devoted entirely to marketing or to the sections of a business plan devoted to marketing.

A Flexible Approach: Three Types of Marketing Plans

While marketing plans tend to be conceived according to each individual company's needs, it is possible to categorize them broadly. These categorizations are linked most closely to the stage and most pressing challenges of the company's business. Using the marketing plans of the companies featured in this book, I have come up with three broad categorizations of marketing plans:

For a new company, the key marketing challenge is simply to understand such fundamentals as the dynamics of the market, the motivations of prospective customers, and the company's place in that market—the ingredients of strategy.

1. Start-up or early-stage strategic plan.

The issue of implementation is by necessity going to get less attention. Indeed, it could be counterproductive to try to lock an early-stage company into a detailed implementation approach when the overall strategy could be flawed in one way or another. A more sensible approach involves testing ways for getting customers to buy. For instance, which of several distribution approaches might work best? Or which of a few promotional strategies might have the best payback?

R.W. Frookies' plan is of this type. It devotes much of its effort to explaining in narrative form, with backup statistics and quotes from credible journals and experts, the then-existing state of the cookie industry and the rising concern among consumers about sugar consumption. It also provides an overview of its anticipated key competitors.

Implementation in the form of distribution and promotional support is both specific and speculative. The company had already lined up three credible distributors in the Northeast but beyond that, there were possibilities but no definite commitments. Also, the pace of expansion was expected to be at the rate of one new urban market area each year. But, of course, that might need to be sped up or slowed down depending on actual experience.

2. Aggressive growth strategic-implementation plan.

Once a company has developed a strategy that seems to be working, it can give renewed emphasis to implementation issues. It can assess more closely its past implementation tactics, determine which work best, and seek to exploit those more effectively. It can seek feedback from prospects and customers about which approaches work best and how they can be improved upon.

A marketing plan that focuses on strategy and implementation usually has two characteristics that distinguish it from the start-up or early-stage strategic plan. For one thing, the strategic-implementation plan is usually closely linked with financial matters. There are detailed budgets and projected revenues from various distribution and sales channels, determined on a monthly or quarterly basis. For another, these plans are often narrowly focused according to product or service line. Thus, each of several products or services will have its own marketing plan.

The two marketing plans for Wall Street Games that I examine deal with both strategy and implementation, with emphasis on the latter. Of one plan's 18 pages, 7 are financial spreadsheets dealing with the costs of marketing materials, expenses associated with various distribution techniques, and projected contribution to overhead of various sales channels.

The two plans each deal with a particular service line—the Fourth Annual AT&T Collegiate Investment Challenge and the annual National Investment Challenge. The first is directed at college and high school students and the second at the general population. Other service lines involving investments and sports have their own marketing plans. This approach allows the company to mobilize its executives and employees around highly focused marketing approaches. It also lets them measure their performance from year to year according to the parameters laid out by the plan.

Companies with well-established, proven marketing strategies may well decide to devote their market planning efforts primarily to implementation issues. What is working and what isn't, and what new approaches might be called for to make the basic strategy work more effectively?

Syms, the off-price retailer, is a classic case of a well-established company that devotes itself to fine-tuning its implementation approach. The company has been in business since 1959, when Sy Syms opened his first store selling irregular and overstock brand-name clothing. For the first 15 years, as the company gradually expanded to five

3. Mature-company implementation plan.

Marketing Plan Sample Table of Contents

Strategic Issues

I.   The Market: Overview
II. Market Strategy
III. Market Position
IV. Competitive Assessment

Implementation Issues

V.   Using Information and Technology
VI. Budgets
VII. Timetables and Management

stores in New York and New Jersey, the company's marketing approach was based nearly entirely on word-of-mouth promotion.

In 1974 Sy Syms got an opportunity to do a 60-second radio spot in exchange for providing a gift certificate to football players being interviewed on a show. He decided to use the time to explain various aspects of retailing and discounting—how department stores set prices at double the manufacturer's price and how Syms obtained overstocks at low prices and reduced prices every ten days that an item stayed on the shelves. The approach worked and gradually Syms fine-tuned its radio and television commercials as it expanded to 36 stores by 1994.

By the early 1990s, Syms's marketing strategy was well established, combining word of mouth and radio-tele-

vision commercials featuring Sy Syms explaining, "An educated consumer is our best customer."

According to Marcy Syms, president of the chain, the
company focuses its marketing primarily on refining its
advertising program. For instance, Syms gradually
reduced its budget for such advertising to 1.75% of the previous year's gross sales from the 2.5% it used in the early
and mid-1980s. "We've pared down our advertising as markets have changed," she says. "We think at some point,
word of mouth goes up and advertising goes down." In
other words, as the company becomes well established in
its new markets, the need for advertising decreases.

The company devotes much attention to targeting the
kinds of shows it advertises on, she says, based on its marketing strategy of "selling brand-name clothes at far below
cost, rather than cheap clothes." Thus, the company seeks
upscale consumers who are more likely to watch a football
game than a show featuring bowling. The company's written
implementation plan, then, consists of single-page schedules
of the shows the company advertises on in each of its urban
markets (one page is excerpted at the end of Chapter 10).

What Should the Marketing Plan Cover?

Clearly, there is no single table of contents that applies to all marketing
plans. Just as there are different types of marketing plans, so there are different subjects that can be addressed.

Basically, each plan, no matter what the labels given to each topic, must focus on identifying key issues, mobilizing resources, and measuring results. Beyond that, the specific subjects to be addressed are up to you, based on your business situation and priorities. Some suggestions can be offered, based on the previous section.

If your business is at the start-up stage, you most likely want to focus on strategic issues and test out possible implementation approaches. If your company is well established and growing quickly, you probably want to give equal emphasis to both strategic and implementation matters.

The actual form the marketing plan takes isn't essential. It's important that it is conceived and structured to enable the company to accomplish its most pressing marketing tasks.

To provide you with some suggestions for structuring your plan, I have listed the marketing subjects covered in three company plans (see the exhibits at the end of this chapter). A perusal of the topics provides a good indication of each company's marketing priorities. For instance, a significant part of R.W. Frookies' plan explains how the company stacks up in a market with lots of well-heeled competitors. Wall Street Games places a high priority on quantitative and technological issues such as finance, operations, and management information systems (MIS). CareerTrack is clearly preoccupied with targeting its growth.

I have also listed in the box on page 52 the subjects a complete marketing plan should address. They are divided according to strategic and implementation matters and serve as a preview to the remainder of this book.

A useful approach is to review these listings and consider which ones your marketing plan should deal with. Use the answers you provided to the exercises in Chapter 1 and the first draft of the marketing overview in the exercise in Chapter 2.

▶ **Exercises**

1. Which of the three types of marketing plans do you feel is most appropriate for your company to prepare?

2. Do you need more than one plan and, if so, which products/services should they cover?

3. Using the material you wrote in answer to the exercise questions in Chapters 1 and 2, and your answer to Question 1 above, list the six most pressing marketing questions facing your company at its current stage of development.

4. From your answers to Questions 1 and 3 above, develop a tentative table of contents for your company's marketing plan.

5. Determine how you will go about writing the marketing plan. What is your schedule for completing the plan?

(Worksheets for this chapter are provided on page 275)

EXHIBIT 3-1

R.W. FROOKIES
MARKETING SUBJECTS COVERED

The Market
> An Overview
> The Soft Cookie
> The Opportunity: Where is the healthy, good-tasting cookie?

The Competition
> Nabisco
> Archway
> Pepperidge Farm
> Barbara's Cookies
> Pride of the Farm
> Nature's Warehouse
> Famous Amos
> A Final Comment: Pricing and the Competition

Marketing and Distribution

Discussion of Financial Projections
> Market Penetration
> Pricing
> Costs
> Projections and Future Financial Goals

EXHIBIT 3-2

FROM THE MARKETING PLAN OF ★WALL STREET GAMES★

3

The Best Plan for You

WALL STREET GAMES
MARKETING SUBJECTS COVERED

(Collegiate Investment Challenge)

Overview

New and Improved for 1991
      Corporate Sponsorship
      Junior Achievement and DECA
      Registration and Survey Information

Finance

Agency

MIS

Public Relations

Operations

FROM THE MARKETING PLAN OF
★ CAREERTRACK ★

EXHIBIT 3-3

CAREERTRACK
MARKETING SUBJECTS COVERED

Growth Prospects
New Seminar Topics
International Expansion
Increased Publications Sales
Additional Private, On-Site Seminars
Growth of Customer List Rental Income
New Product/Market Development

Strengths/Competitive Advantages

Industry and Competition

PART II:

DEVISING A STRATEGY

THE MARKET

*Understanding
the Big Picture*

As I discussed in previous chapters, there are few industries not undergoing major changes. Increased competition, government regulation, newly emerging technology, internationalization, and rapidly changing customer tastes are among the factors affecting many industries. In such a turbulent business environment, it's imperative that you have a clear and informed overview of the marketplace. To understand the big picture is to make sense of the world around you—specifically, by examining your industry and where it's going and how the outside world is affecting your industry.

Your Industry and Where It's Going

You need total familiarity with your industry to assess your marketing prospects realistically. You also want to know how the strategy you develop compares with what others in the industry are doing so you don't take approaches that can't work based on industry trends or structure, or devise approaches that have already been tried.

Here are some questions to consider:

• Is demand for your product/ service growing or shrinking?

Ideally, you want to be in a growing market so your company will grow with the market. In the R.W. Frookies marketing plan (see Exhibit 4–1 on page 82), Richard Worth plays to this desire when he observes: "Frookies will compete in the United States cookie market, a giant segment which had total sales in 1985 of over $4 billion. The trend has been towards steady increases in sales volume and prices: cookie consumption climbed to 11 pounds per capita in 1985, up from 10.5 pounds the year earlier. Retail prices also increased by about 3% in 1985."

But two points should be noted regarding demand: First, being in a growing market does not ensure your company will succeed, because growing markets tend to attract many competitors. By the same token, being in a shrinking market doesn't mean you are doomed to failure. Declining demand often means that competitors are abandoning a market, creating opportunities for companies with innovative approaches to serve customers.

The declining-demand scenario is dealt with in CareerTrack's 1992 marketing plan overview (see Exhibit 4–2 on page 85). In the second paragraph, the plan points out that "the $43.2 billion spent on training in 1991 represents a 5% decrease from 1990."

The question facing the company's management, then, is whether this is part of a long-term decline. The next sentence makes clear management's belief that the change was an aberration, explaining that much of the decline was the result of recession-related budget cutting. And the following paragraph points out, "Indications are that the training industry will rebound slightly in 1992."

• What has been the long-term change?

As CareerTrack's plan makes clear, it is difficult to make definite judgments based on year-to-year changes in demand. A 5% decline in demand one year could be an ominous sign or a recession-caused blip. To avoid being misled, executives must examine longer-term trends.

Many plans fail to consider the past to get a meaningful indication of what the real trend is. CareerTrack's plan seeks to put the 5% decline in training expenditures into perspective by noting in the fifth paragraph the change during the last 10 to 20 years from in-house to externally provided training.

• Why has the change taken place?

Explaining industry trends is essential to understanding their implications for your company. This is another area that tends to get little attention in many plans, in part because it is often difficult to determine or the explanations are complex.

If you ask newspaper publishers why the number of daily newspapers has declined since the 1940s, their responses include the impact of television, the declining quality of

4

The Market

our schools, shortened attention spans, reduced interest in reading, the movement of the middle class to the suburbs, and so on. Those who conclude the problem is television and shortened attention spans may try to counter it by reducing the length of newspaper articles, which some have done, with encouraging results. Those who decide the problem is the exodus to the suburbs could come out with suburban editions, and indeed, some have done that. And those who conclude that reduced interest in reading is the problem may conclude they are fighting a losing battle and continue doing what they have always done or sell out. The reasons you decide are most valid, then, will have an important impact on your marketing strategy.

CareerTrack's marketing plan doesn't explain the long-term trend away from in-house company training and toward outside training. The implication for the company is clear, though: Overall expenditures on training may have declined 5% from one year to the next, but the trend over the last decade or two is toward using outside training services. In that context, a 5% decline in overall expenditures, whether it's a short-term blip or the beginning of a longer-term change, doesn't seem ominous.

Beyond that, though, it would be helpful to know whether the long-term change is companies' response to financial pressure, a recognition that outsiders provide more effective training, or some other factors. Then the company might be able to design other innovative products and services to capitalize on the change.

Every industry can be divided into various segments, or categories. In the newspaper industry, for instance, there are daily and weekly newspapers; metropolitan, suburban, and rural newspapers; and business and industry newspapers. These categories overlap (i.e., weekly industry newspapers).

R.W. Frookies describes itself as being in the "soft cookie" segment. Its plan describes the evolution of this segment, beginning in 1983, when "Duncan Hines launched a massive campaign to promote a 'new' product, the soft cookie. With a softer texture, the cookie was designed as a 'homestyle alternative' to the mass-produced cookies which had not changed since the 1950s."

That kind of cookie encountered problems in measuring up to consumers' quality expectations, notes the plan. Frookies is thus positioned as "a soft cookie which—first and foremost—tastes good."

In its plan, CareerTrack also refers to its segment of the training industry by pointing out that it has sought to establish a new segment counter to the industry's tradition:

"Prior to CareerTrack's inception, seminar providers generally sought to educate relatively small groups on a high individual-fee basis. The Company's success has revealed the demand for lower-priced, larger-audience seminars which recognize time and monetary constraints, yet provide effective training."

• **What kind of segmentation has taken place?**

4

The Market

• What is the industry's "system"?

Each industry has its established approaches to distribution, promotion, and selling, along with special criteria to describe marketing success. In retailing, success is often measured in sales per square foot. In the mail-order-catalog business, key yardsticks are responses per thousand catalogs sent and the average order size per response.

Your marketing plan should discuss and analyze your industry practices and how they affect your company. It is not necessary that your company stick with all the practices, but if it plans to do things differently, these should be explained.

Anita Roddick understood the cosmetics industry's way of doing things, and decided that The Body Shop would do things differently. She notes in her book, *Body and Soul,* "that my instinctive trading values were diametrically opposed to the business practices of the cosmetics industry in just about every area." She then proceeds to list ten practices she opposed, including an emphasis on packaging, testing products on animals, spending huge sums on advertising, and pushing "beauty products; I banished the word 'beauty'." Another key: emphasizing high-quality products in an industry that seemed to regard products as secondary to image.

• Where is the industry headed?

No one, of course, can provide a definitive answer for any industry. But the question should be addressed in the overview of the market. A useful way to consider it is to incorporate the projections of recognized experts.

In its marketing overview R.W. Frookies does a good job of considering the future when it states: "The future appears promising for all the players. One trade analyst, Packaged Facts Inc., has projected that the cookie market will grow by 10% annually to $6.5 billion in 1990. Most of this new growth is expected to be from adults, to whom new cookies are now being marketed. Until recently, consumption and selection had been dominated by children."

This prediction not only provides an industry sales projection, but the possibilities for a long-term change in industry trends—from children guiding cookie selection to adults becoming the driving force. Such a fundamental change, of course, has significant implications to those in the industry shrewd enough to recognize it. Frookies management is aware of the trend and can factor it into the company's strategy.

How the Outside World Affects Your Industry

Once you have a clear understanding of the trends at work in your industry, you need to consider them in the context of broader national and international trends. Here are some of the more important ones:

• The economy. I'm not referring to the economy in terms that the media usually discuss it—whether it is headed up or down. I am talking about the impact of overall economic trends.

For instance, the fact that U.S. workers' productivity did not grow enough in the 1970s and 1980s to raise living standards has made many companies receptive to productivity-improvement products and services. It has also made them less tolerant of hiring such professionals as lawyers, accountants, and consultants unless executives can see evidence of tangible financial payback.

The failure of living standards to rise appreciably during the same period put a squeeze on the middle class, making it more value conscious in its purchases. That economic fact of life has no doubt aided Syms and a variety of other off-price chains.

• **Government policy.**

On a national scale, it is easy to see how government actions can have a major impact on entire industries. Deregulation of the airline industry wound up creating conditions in which such major carriers as Pan Am and Eastern couldn't survive. It also opened up opportunities for many upstarts, some of which also didn't survive. The talk among Presidential candidates during the 1992 election campaign and the many proposals initiated in Congress about reforming the health-care system had executives in and out of the health-care field asking themselves how the various approaches to governmental involvement would affect them.

On a local level, government regulations can have significant effects. The tough environmental regulations enacted in California and New Jersey have raised the cost of doing business for some manufacturers—and raised the question of whether they should move their operations to other states. The movement by states to collect sales taxes from residents on mail-order items purchased from out-of-state companies has had a major impact on direct-mail companies.

Smart executives are aware of such changes, and they factor the potential long-term impact into their marketing plans.

The values that consumers and businesspeople hold dear are constantly changing. For instance, the media during the early 1990s was full of articles about how consumers had shifted from conspicuous consumption toward saving. The implications of this change were far-reaching for businesses ranging from banks to automakers to food companies.

• Cultural and social values.

For Wall Street Games, for instance, such a change has potentially favorable implications because consumers use its pretend-investing format to practice for the real thing. And CareerTrack's low-cost seminars provide a double-barrel advantage: a way to obtain the training necessary to get ahead at the lowest possible cost.

But other values are also important: The growing concern about health has created opportunities for companies selling organic foods and vitamin supplements, and created problems for businesses selling junk food and liquor. But within such problems lie opportunities as well, as Ken

69

Meyers and Richard Worth demonstrated with Smartfoods and R.W. Frookies—take an unhealthful product and make it look healthful. Increasing concern about the environment has helped companies making biodegradable soaps and garbage bags. Smart executives like Anita Roddick of The Body Shop have also capitalized on the trend by demonstrating their concern about the environment and giving consumers opportunities to help. At Body Shop stores, customers are encouraged to recycle the company's plastic containers.

• **Lifestyle trends.**

Economic, social, and other trends typically have a significant effect on lifestyles. Among the major trends of recent years have been the movement of women into the work force and the growing level of crime in U.S. society. The impact of each on lifestyles is readily apparent. Women have less time to shop and thus value the convenience afforded by such things as mail-order clothing and take-out or microwavable food. The rise in crime has been a boon to a variety of businesses, from burglar alarm companies to video stores, as consumers try not only to protect themselves but also to avoid venturing onto city streets after dark. Conversely, both trends have had a negative impact on many long-established retailers, especially those in the downtowns of major cities.

These trends can also be seen to benefit companies featured in this book. Students who can store and prepare snacks in the MicroFridge appliance avoid the inconvenience, and the threat of crime, of going out late at night. Similarly, Wall Street Games is part of a growing trend to seek different yet convenient entertainment, all obtained within the privacy of one's home.

Where you are located or operating your business can make an important difference. Most obviously, swimming pools sell better in Florida than in Massachusetts and ski equipment will do better in Massachusetts than in Florida.

• Geography.

Geography can have more subtle marketing implications, though, that may be difficult to anticipate. For instance, companies selling educational products like textbooks often encounter widely varying approval and selection processes from state to state.

Smartfoods discovered another aspect when it became the dominant snack food in New England in the mid- and late 1980s. The fact that its most significant competitors were national in scope or strong in other regions put it at a disadvantage. Between 1986 and 1989, recalls Ken Meyers, "A ridiculous flood of me-too products came at us. Many of them were targeted specifically to just knock us off." Indeed, he notes that "we were effectively preempted in most of the markets outside New England by these competitors, either regional or national players." Smartfoods still managed to do well in many of the non–New England markets, but the intensity of the competition eventually helped convince the company to sell out to Frito Lay.

• Technological change.

The speed with which technology is changing has a major impact on all kinds of businesses. One obvious example has been the effect of the personal computer on companies in the computer industry. Makers of minicomputers and mainframe computers, like Digital Equipment and IBM, were caught off guard by the inroads personal computers and desktop systems made into major corporations—and experienced severe financial losses as a result.

Executives who anticipate the effects of technological change can benefit enormously. Tim DeMello has successfully exploited the availability of microcomputers and other technology to replicate the functions of a major brokerage firm.

The company's equivalent of "brokers" are college students in front of computer terminals who instantaneously call up the records of participants in a Collegiate Investment Challenge as they phone in and execute stock trades. Each record has additional information about how the source came to Wall Street Games—whether through direct-mail promotion, a particular television commercial, a newspaper ad, a college bulletin board, or word of mouth—so the company can determine which approaches work best and adjust its future promotions. Sophisticated tape machines record each call so it can be listened to if there are disputes about the timing and specifics of a transaction. The technology provides competitive advantages as well, which are discussed in Chapter 7. "We've placed a high priority on making use of all the wonderful technology that is available, and it has paid us back in spades," says DeMello.

Get the Answers You Need

Chances are, you can't immediately provide answers or explanations to deal with all the issues raised in this chapter. If you've been involved in a particular industry, you may know where to get the answers. If you haven't, you face a bigger, but not impossible, challenge.

The task at hand is commonly referred to as market research. Here are some sources for getting the answers you need:

A useful first step, even for those with experience in an industry, is to search out recent articles about your industry. Computerized databases make such searches quick and fairly painless. Many public libraries do the searches for little or no charge. Otherwise, you are probably best off asking your librarian for the names of consultants who specialize in doing database searches. You can attempt them yourself via one of the many computerized data services like CompuServe, but it may be more time-consuming and expensive than using a consultant.

• Articles and studies.

A database search usually provides one-paragraph summaries of articles and industry studies. If you want more detail, you can photocopy the original article or contact the organization that conducted the study to obtain it. (Be warned, some consulting firms charge several hundred or even a few thousand dollars for a specialized industry study.)

The articles and studies will likely provide further leads. For instance, they often cite industry experts you may want to contact. Or there may be references to court cases you will want to probe further; the documents in most court cases are open to the public.

Another excellent resource for industry assessments is investment studies. Many brokerage firms research a number of industries, along with the companies in each industry. Value Line regularly examines dozens of industries to consider their growth prospects and potential problems, and it is available in many libraries.

• Competitive assessment.

I devote Chapter 7 to the matter of competition, but in the context of market research, you can learn a great deal about your industry by observing what competitors do. The best ways to do this early on in the market planning process are to examine publicly held companies and attend trade shows.

Because publicly held companies must disclose much financial, personnel, and market data to satisfy Securities and Exchange Commission requirements, a great deal of information is readily available. Their quarterly and annual reports can be a treasure trove of data about new products, customer reaction to existing products, and market trends. These reports can be accessed via databases or at libraries of university business schools.

Trade shows enable you to see in action some of the latest products and services of public and private companies. They also allow you to question company personnel in related or competing businesses about their views of the marketplace.

What you observe in an industry and how you feel about the experience can be extremely important sources of market research. Anita Roddick's unhappiness about the beauty industry's direction has been a driving force in establishing and growing The Body Shop. She points out in *Body and Soul* her feeling that the cosmetics business is heavily oriented toward selling youth at a time when large segments of the world population are growing old and require new products for their aging skin. She notes that the cosmetics industry is "too busy creating products that no one needs, too busy trying to persuade women that they need not grow old."

• Your own experience.

Roddick's own observations about the industry's direction—or misdirection, in her view—have driven her to formulate products for an aging population. She assessed the cosmetics marketplace and concluded from studying the ads, shopping, and looking at various products that the industry was overlooking an important trend. The Body Shop has devoted considerable research to developing products to serve the needs of the elderly, according to Roddick.

She also made the observation that the cosmetics industry plays fast and loose with the truth. "I hate the beauty business," Roddick says. "It is a monster industry selling unattainable dreams. It lies. It cheats. It exploits women." In that context, she wanted her business to be the industry's antithesis.

Many of your employees have important information and insights about the market. Salespeople tend to be in

• Your employees.

75

closest contact with customers, prospects, and competitors, but many others in your company also have information. Secretaries, receptionists, and clerks hear comments from customers that may provide important clues about changing industry practices or expectations.

The challenge is to mine this source. One way is to chat informally with employees and ask them specifically what they are hearing. Another is to encourage them to fill out brief forms or notes about what they are hearing. The prospect of a bonus or other financial incentive for information judged the most useful can encourage employees to keep tabs of what they learn.

Putting the Pieces Together

Your challenge is to put together all the information you gathered in an organized and meaningful way. Based on what you have found out about the world around you, how should your marketing approach or strategy be altered?

Because you likely have a mountain of information and knowledge at this point, it is easy to feel overwhelmed. Here are some questions that can help you use this information most advantageously:

• Are the changes you have observed a trend or a fad?

A trend is indicative of something much more far-reaching and permanent than a fad. It can be said, though, that a fad such as teenage boys carving their initials into their scalp is possibly indicative of a trend toward more individuality. To mistake a fad for a trend can be dangerous because you may make decisions with long-term implications for your business based on erroneous information.

As we know from basic physics, for every action, there is a reaction. Most obviously, when the auto manufacturers slump, an assortment of other businesses are affected, from the bars and grills surrounding the plants to the parts suppliers to makers of steel and rubber. Similarly, when newspaper sales rise or fall, demand for paper and related manufacturing equipment is affected. Marketing experts refer to this phenomenon as derived demand.

The effects can be less obvious, however. Many owners of movie theaters—from drive-ins to "adult" theaters—failed to appreciate the significance of videocassettes until it was too late for their businesses. And many supermarkets have been caught off guard by the emergence of membership discount chains such as Costco and BJ's.

• Are there ripple effects in your market?

Most product categories go through a cycle during which demand initially is slow, picks up, peaks, levels off, and declines. The product life cycle, as it is known to marketers, is represented graphically by a bell curve. One example is the color television. When the first color models came on the market around 1960, they were expensive and of questionable quality. By the 1970s, color television became the norm and sales skyrocketed. By the 1980s, sales had leveled off. In anticipation of the inevitable decline, manufacturers came out with new categories such

• Where is your product (or service) in the product life cycle?

4

The Market

as big-screen and stereo models, and began looking ahead to high-definition models.

Executives need to be sure that a product area that looks solid now isn't on the far side of the bell curve. They also need to be aware that product life cycles are shortening. Products that once could be counted on for a five- or six-year life cycle may now only have three or four years.

• What are the likely scenarios for your market?

A useful exercise is to imagine likely occurrences in your marketplace. Try for a minimum of three and preferably more. One can be the conventional wisdom scenario that many of the industry experts are projecting, a second can be a more radical one, and a third a conservative scenario. For health-care companies trying to anticipate the future during the 1990s, one conventional scenario is increased government involvement, including mandating that employers and insurance companies make health insurance more widely available and set limits on the prices of prescription drugs. A more radical scenario would be national health insurance. A very conservative expectation would be that insurance companies, drug companies, and other major players introduce some internal reform that keeps the system the way it was in the early 1990s. There are, of course, other scenarios that can be devised, based on the many proposals put forth.

Executives must determine the impact on their product or service based on each scenario. Taking a health-care scenario and applying it to a small testing lab, national health insurance could be great because it would enlarge the market by providing access to health care for more than 35 million Americans who have no coverage. Conversely, the controls of national health insurance might reduce the prices a lab could charge or place limitations on doctors to order tests, adversely affecting profits. Going through the exercise forces you to use the market research in ways you may not have thought about.

This is probably the hardest question to answer. Basically, it requires you to look at all the information you've assembled and find things that seem inconsistent or illogical. Many law firms during the mid- and late 1980s failed to understand the discontinuity associated with the fact that they were feverishly expanding their practices and raising their hourly rates at a time when many corporations were downsizing or, at a minimum, reexamining their expenses. Eventually, many firms paid a steep price when they were caught with expensive overhead in a declining market.

Discontinuities aren't always major occurrences, but they can carry important signals. For example, consumer interest in organic foods during the 1970s and 1980s seemed a peripheral fancy and was ignored by many in the food industry. But the interest signaled concerns about the safety and healthfulness of the food we eat, and those processors, supermarket chains, fast-food franchisers, and others that realized its relevance have capitalized on it— including R.W. Frookies and Smartfoods.

• What are the discontinuities in the marketplace?

4

The Market

Businesses that have the most difficulty recognizing discontinuities tend to be those with a long, stable tradition. They tend to arrogantly disregard discontinuities. Many of the companies that made vacuum tubes that powered electronic goods during the 1940s and 1950s were caught off guard by the implications of the transistor and, later, by the semiconductor chip. U.S. auto companies ignored Japanese and German automakers for too long. Such failures can cost companies dearly.

Executives who recognize discontinuities often must be prepared to make major changes in the way they do business. Computer companies that want to survive have had to adjust to a merging of various media, including video, audio, and telephone. The worst thing a company can do is ignore discontinuities, because they are a principal source of marketing surprises. And the last thing you want in today's marketplace is to be surprised.

Even after you've done all the things advocated here, you still won't know for certain where the market is headed. The real goal in assessing the environment is to reduce the chances of being surprised. Doing that increases the odds in your favor.

▶ **Exercises**

1. Describe the overall financial direction of your industry over the last 10 to 20 years.

2. Describe the three most important trends that have affected your industry over the last 10 to 20 years.

3. Which industry segment does your company operate in?

4. Describe briefly how you expect the following to affect your company:

   • **The economy**

   • **Government policy**

   • **Cultural and social values**

   • **Lifestyle trends**

   • **Geography**

   • **Technological change**

5. Graphically chart the product life cycle of each of your company's products and services, as far as can be determined. Using what has happened until now, project the rest of the cycle.

6. Describe at least three possible scenarios for your industry and explain how each would most likely affect your position in the marketplace.

7. Identify at least one discontinuity affecting your industry and describe how it could affect your company.

(Worksheets for this chapter are provided on page 278)

EXHIBIT 4–1

THE MARKET

An Overview

Frookies will compete in the United States cookies market, a giant segment which had total sales in 1985 of over $4 billion.[1] The trend has been towards steady increases in sales volume and prices: cookie consumption climbed to 11 pounds per capita in 1985, up from 10.5 pounds the year earlier.[2] Retail prices also increased by about 3% in 1985.

Retailers purchased 90% of the 2.1 billion pounds of cookies produced in 1985.[3] Although convenience stores hold significant potential for growth, over 70% of all cookies are purchased through supermarkets. There are 126,000 supermarkets in the United States, of which 30,000 are considered to be major stores. In 1985, "store-door delivered cookies" had 169 average linear feet of shelf space in major supermarkets—the second largest physical space required for a product behind only soft drinks.[4]

Overall, the cookie market has been dominated by the large producers such as Nabisco, Keebler, and Duncan Hines. The largest seller in the category, the Oreo, is 76 years old. More recently, a number of new entrants such as the gourmet cookie (i.e. Famous Amos) have been successfully introduced. The

[1] "Cookie Sales Start Rolling Up Super Numbers," *Grocery Marketing*, February 1987, p. 39.
[2] Mark Gaynor, "Bakers Make Crucial Choices as America Changes Face," *Bakery*, May 1986, p. 87.
[3] Mark Gaynor, p. 87.
[4] "1986 Neilsen Review of Retail Store Trends," *Progressive Grocer*, September 1986, p. 13.

—————— E X H I B I T 4 – 1 ——————
continued

future appears promising for all the players. One trade analyst, Packaged Facts Inc., has projected that the cookie market will grow by 10% annually to $6.5 billion in 1990. Most of this new growth is expected to be from adults, to whom new cookies are now being marketed. Until recently, consumption and selection had been dominated by children.[5]

The Soft Cookie

Although cookie sales overall have been strong, the recent "soft cookie wars" demonstrate that consumers might be somewhat bored by the current offerings, and in any event, are certainly willing to forsake brand loyalty and try something new.

In 1983, Duncan Hines launched a massive campaign to promote a "new" product, the soft cookie. With a softer texture, the cookie was designed as a "homestyle alternative" to the mass-produced cookies which had not changed since the 1950s.

The consumer and competitor response was immediate. Keebler, Nabisco, and Frito Lay all came out with their own versions of soft cookies. The sales of conventional "hard" cookies dropped substantially as consumers opted to try the newer, different cookie. Millions were spent on advertising and the soft cookie was projected to grab a 35% share of the entire cookie market.[6]

The soft cookie was an enormous flop. Duncan Hines has recently cut back its production substantially after incurring $265

5 *Grocery Marketing*, p. 39.

million in pre-tax losses between 1984 and 1986. Nabisco and Keebler have dramatically reduced their expectations and the soft cookie now has only a 10-15% share of the cookie market.[7]

What happened? According to one consultant who closely followed the soft cookie wars, "the package tasted better than the product." Another senior executive at one company pointed out that "The selling point was texture, not flavor."[8]

The soft cookie episode certainly demonstrates that the consumer will try a new product. Interestingly enough, the major manufacturers all emphasize "wholesome" names and themes in their advertising campaigns—such as "Grandma's" (Frito Lay), and "Almost Home" (Nabisco). The cookies, however, were not as good as promised and consumers returned to the more conventional cookies.

By contrast, Frookies will be a soft cookie which—first and foremost—tastes good. Through the use of wholesome ingredients (and no sugar) Frookies will be able to deliver on the "all natural and wholesome" themes that were promised by the competitors in the soft cookie wars.

EXHIBIT 4-2

FROM THE MARKETING PLAN OF
★ *CAREERTRACK* ★

INDUSTRY

Each year, individuals and employers seek reputable outside training resources to gain and upgrade skills in an increasingly competitive business environment. As a result, training has become a very large, diverse and rapidly growing industry. According to *Training* magazine's annual industry report (October 1991), U.S. organizations with 100 or more employees spent an estimated $43.2 billion on training in 1991. Outside-the-company training services accounted for about $12.3 billion of the total expenditures, with internal training staff salaries accounting for the balance.

Of the $43.2 billion, 6% or $2.5 billion was spent on seminars and conferences. Off-the-shelf materials (books, tapes, films, computer "courseware") account for another $1.3 billion, or 3% of the total. Growth estimates for the business seminar segment and off-the-shelf segments are not available. However, the $43.2 billion spent on training in 1991 represents a 5% decrease from 1990. Conversely, according to *Training*'s report, half the organizations they surveyed cut back budgets or reduced their number of employees as a result of the 1990-91 recession. In one-fourth of those budgets where training was cut, it was cut equally with other budget line items.

Indications are that the training industry will rebound slightly in 1992. The *Training* magazine survey showed that 88% of the companies interviewed expected their training expenditures to increase or stay the same in 1992 (only 12% expect a decline).

For the second consecutive year, videotape programs are pre-

EXHIBIT 4-2

continued

dicted to be the most popular instructional medium. CareerTrack has a significant presence in this market, as one of the top five audio and videotape publishers in the world. *Training*'s survey estimated that 90% of the organizations surveyed use videotape as a training vehicle. In addition, seminar lectures proved popular, with 85% of responding companies using them. Audiotapes were used by 51% of the respondents.

Another important factor in the business seminar industry is that only about 10% of training and development needs are met exclusively through in-house training departments. Employers look outside their organizations to meet the vast majority of their training and development needs. In contrast, 10 to 20 years ago, only a small portion of training requirements were met by outside sources. Our records show that tuition costs for 89% of our public-seminar attendees are paid for by their employers.

Prior to CareerTrack's inception, seminar providers generally sought to educate relatively small groups on a high individual-fee basis. The Company's success has revealed the demand for lower-priced, larger-audience seminars which recognize time and money constraints, yet provide effective training.

In the U.S. alone, about 36.8 million employees are expected to spend a total of 1.22 billion hours in some type of formal training process this year. Management skills, communication skills and customer relations/service are among the most popular training topics.

Challenges faced by training and development organizations for the next two to five years include creating new market strategies and organizational missions, exceptional customer service and establishing a corporate culture. CareerTrack is ideally positioned to meet those challenges through its products and services.

MARKETING STRATEGY

*What are
Your Customers
REALLY Buying?*

If I asked you to describe briefly what the companies profiled in this book sell, you would have little problem providing answers. Smartfoods sells cheddar cheese popcorn. The Body Shop sells natural cosmetics. Syms sells off-price clothing. CareerTrack sells seminars. MicroFridge sells a combination microwave oven-refrigerator-freezer. Frookies sells healthful cookies. Wall Street Games sells a mock investment game.

If only it were that simple! If I asked you why these companies have been more successful selling their particular products than competitors selling the same or similar products, you might be harder pressed to explain. You might attribute Smartfoods' success to its high quality, or CareerTrack's to its low price. But other companies have tried similar formulas with the same product or service and been unable to duplicate the success of Smartfoods and CareerTrack. The reason these and other companies prosper is that what you see isn't always what you get.

When you look at the big picture as recommended in the last chapter, you should develop a strategy that gets to the marketing essence of your product or service. That essence needs to be stated in terms of what the customer is really buying.

The marketing essence of a product or service is often something that in retrospect seems obvious. But pinpointing it requires deep familiarity with your market as discussed in the previous chapter, and even deeper thinking about it. Bob Bennett's realization that what MicroFridge was really selling wasn't an appliance but a way to help customers increase revenues and profits—for instance, managers of university dormitories could hold onto students who might otherwise move out to apartments—was based on his intimate knowledge and study of the market. It seems simplistic when stated that way but, as a matter of strategy, it is quite sophisticated and has become a driving force in the company's success.

What Are You Really Selling?

Answering this in a true marketing-oriented way is one of the most difficult challenges facing any executive. Your response guides your overall approach to identifying prospects and convincing them to buy. The more off target you are, the greater the difficulty you will have in devising a marketing strategy that works. Conversely, the more clearly you understand what customers want, the more likely you will be able to ensure they get it.

Too often, executives define their product in terms of quality or price. A restaurant owner says he or she has the best hamburgers or pizza. A secretarial service claims it has the most reliable data-entry people. A software company contends its programs have the most complete array of features. And, of course, all these top-quality products or services are available at attractive prices.

The problem with such claims is that everyone in your industry is making similar ones. You must understand on a deeper level what customers are seeking.

McDonald's understood that people were less concerned with the quality of its hamburgers than with how quick and cheap they are. Similarly, Domino's Pizza has long realized that its business is more about fast delivery than pizza quality.

Both businesses offer an additional factor: the comfort of knowing that the hamburger or pizza in Buffalo is the same as the one in Atlanta or San Diego. When families travel and are feeling anxious about being in a strange place, they can still find some familiar, known products. Parents who go into a McDonald's or order a Domino's pizza don't have to worry about an evening being ruined by a child complaining, "This hamburger tastes funny," or "Why is the pizza taking so long?"

So it might be said that McDonald's and Domino's sell convenience at an affordable price and sell a form of insurance against receiving an unpleasant surprise at mealtime. Those are important features to many people.

When Ken Meyers talks about Smartfood, he talks less about the high quality of the popcorn than about the resentment many people feel when they examine the snack food section of their supermarkets. Most of the foods are "greasy and artificial," he says. "We decided to make a product we could present to the world as the antithesis—smart food to the world's junk food." That is a powerful concept if you carry it through. Consumers get the pleasures of junk food without putrid colors or greasy appearances. Guilt-free junk food is like guilt-free sin. Everyone can relate to that.

Arriving at these kinds of conclusions isn't easy, even for some of the entrepreneurs profiled in this book. If you talk with Anita Roddick and read her book *Body and Soul,* it is difficult to get a straightforward answer to what she believes her customers are really buying.

She begins her book by railing against the established cosmetics industry. Its promises of beauty and youth represent "false hopes and unattainable dreams," she observes. She is the antithesis of the established cosmetics business, she strongly suggests, someone who has no interest in such matters as hype, packaging, profits, or marketing.

But it's difficult to succeed in business simply by being negative about your competitors. So what made Body Shop so successful? "Skill is not the answer, neither is money," she writes. "What you need is optimism, humanism, enthusiasm, intuition, curiosity, love, humor, magic and fun and that secret ingredient—euphoria."

Yet that is not very precise, either. Even though Roddick writes and speaks about marketing with disdain, she may inadvertently describe Body Shop's true marketing strategy when she observes early in her book, "My motivation for going into the cosmetics business was irritation." She didn't like the way the established companies served women—the absence of small sizes for everyday cosmetics, the extensive use of fancy packaging, the exaggerated claims, and the focus on profits.

Her irritation led her to develop an alternative cosmetics business that solved the problems she identified. Her stores sell a variety of sizes, use simply labeled bottles, and provide a great deal of straightforward information about the origins and benefits of the cosmetic ingredients. The focus on the environment and the Third World are an attractive substitute for profits.

Clearly, many other women shared her irritation and identified with the new type of cosmetics business she built, and its alternative dream: beauty based on natural ingredients, along with help for the environment and the Third World. Like Smartfoods, Body Shop allows customers to have their cake and eat it, too. Shopping at a Body Shop relieves the guilt, embarrassment, and anger many feel when they buy traditional cosmetics, while still holding out the hope for an improved appearance.

While Roddick doesn't quite say it that way, she understands that she has struck a chord with many women. She continues to build on her image as an industry nonconformist, vowing to be innovative and different—with a passion that customers can relate to.

The Best Benefits: Your Unique Selling Proposition

The best marketing strategy, then, is stated in the form of benefits to customers. These benefits should not be trivial. Indeed, the more emotionally based and/or financially based they are, the better. (Hitting both emotional and financial hot buttons is ideal.) When you can reduce your marketing strategy to such matters as hope, fear, love, guilt, greed, convenience, increased profits, value pricing, and other emotional or financial issues, you are often on the right track.

Marketing experts sometimes refer to the benefits that enable you to stand apart from the crowd as your unique selling proposition, or USP. A company like Dell Computer was able to carve out a niche for itself in the late 1980s and early 1990s by selling high-quality personal computers at a lower price than many competitors—a USP based on value. Its sales soared.

One company that capitalizes on both emotional and financial benefits is Syms. It promises to save people money by discounting designer or other brand-name clothing. If you want a pair of Walkabout slacks or a Pierre Cardin shirt and can save 25% or 30% of what you'd have paid in a department store, the financial advantage is obvious.

But there is an emotional component to its business as well. When people feel as if they've saved money, they often feel good about themselves. They made smart decisions, shrewd decisions. They proved themselves to be good handlers of money. They can walk out of Syms feeling proud and successful, even if their careers or personal lives are not. They can tell their friends about how much they saved and gain further approval.

All these good feelings may result in spite of the fact that the customer may not have needed the items purchased. Many purchases at Syms (and other discounters) are made by people who need to congratulate themselves on how smart they are to save the kind of money Syms assures them they have saved.

The benefits to Syms are obvious. A customer who leaves a store feeling good is likely to return for a repeat session. And the friends who were impressed may become Syms customers.

• **Emotional benefits.**

Consumer products invariably have an emotional component associated with them. Just watch television commercials to get a sense of the emotional buttons sellers push—ranging from sex (beer ads) to popularity (diet ads) to health (margarine ads).

Wall Street Games relies on a fantasy largely driven by hope. The hope is to win a contest for having the best-performing stock market portfolio. But it is bigger than that, explains founder Tim DeMello: "What we are really doing is giving individuals a realistic experience in a world they couldn't otherwise afford." In other words, for a fee of only $49.95 or $99 (depending on the game), the customer enters the world of the rich Wall Street trader. Suddenly, she has $500,000 (in pretend money) to amass and trade a stock portfolio for three months. Whenever she wants to make a trade, she calls her "broker" at Wall Street Games and gives the order. At the end of three months, a tally is made of all the portfolios to see who has done best—and won real prizes of money.

But the possibility of winning is almost beside the point. What is important to the customer is that for three months, she has been able to experience the lifestyle of the rich and famous. Not a bad deal for $50 or $100.

The Body Shop does something similar. In giving its customers an alternative to traditional cosmetics, it provides a different kind of experience—one featuring natural products; exotic concoctions from faraway lands; a politically correct approach to business; and Third World suppliers like the Kayapo Indians of Brazil, who provide Brazil nuts for use in some products and make jewelry. In other words, there is "the sense of adventure," as Anita Roddick describes it in a brochure (see Exhibit 5–1, page 104) associated with shopping at a Body Shop store.

While consumer products tend to focus on emotional benefits to hook customers, business products typically

• Financial benefits.

93

emphasize financial benefits—making or saving money. Robotic manufacturing equipment is sold because it replaces individual workers and the ongoing salaries they earn. Sophisticated electronic telephone answering and voice mail systems are promoted to replace human telephone operators. Over time, the fax machine is a cheap alternative to overnight-mail services. Various long-distance telephone services compete by claiming to save businesses money. Large stationery supply chains thrive because they save owners of small businesses money.

The amount that a product or service can save in relation to its price can be a powerful selling tool. Coming up with that amount can be an involved process, but well worth the effort. For example, in 1989 Bob Bennett decided that hotels and motels could be an important new market in addition to his original market of college dormitories. One of the attractions of this new market was the compelling financial case that Bennett concluded could be made for use of the MicroFridge in hotel and motel rooms.

Because the MicroFridge appliance gives guests the option to prepare food and snacks in their rooms, it represents both a convenience and a money saver to increasingly cost-conscious travelers. As such, it should be something they would be willing to pay extra for when renting a room, Bennett reasoned.

For hotel and motel managers, then, the MicroFridge unit could be a source of additional revenues. The key question was, how much? Bennett did some calculations, which are reproduced in part in Exhibit 5–2, page 105, to explain and illustrate the benefits to hotel/motel managers.

Bennett's calculations were stressed in his company's marketing plan and for explaining to hotel/motel managers how the MicroFridge appliance can become a separate profit center under a leasing plan. As the benefits description and profit analysis show, hotel/motel managers can earn money from both a surcharge on rooms with the MicroFridge unit as well as from selling microwavable food themselves.

The profit analysis makes quite an attractive case. Over seven years, lease and service charges for 25 MicroFridge units are just a little over $20,000. That expense can be turned into a profit of $158,000 during the same period, according to Bennett's calculations.

But Bennett's profit approach isn't the only way of calculating financial benefits. As part of his test-marketing effort, Bennett solicited endorsements from several hotel/motel managers. He received several back, which are included in MicroFridge's marketing plan; one is reproduced on page 110.

The third to the last paragraph is key. The manager describes the MicroFridge units in terms of paying for themselves. In other words, how long does it take for revenues from the units to pay for the upfront cost? Since this manager purchased the units for $406 each, he saw them taking 58 days of $7 daily room surcharges to pay for themselves.

The implication of the payback is obvious. Once those units have paid for themselves, all additional income is pure gravy. Each MicroFridge unit undergoes a transformation in the hotel/motel manager's mind, going from a simple appliance to a money machine. And who doesn't want a money machine working in his or her business?

Note also that the manager points out the units paid for themselves within six months. That is an excellent payback period. Indeed, any product or service that can pay for itself in less than a year is attractive to a customer, because that isn't a very long time to wait for the birth of a money machine. Two years or less is still attractive, while three years becomes barely acceptable.

It should be noted that these guidelines are most applicable to products or services with short life spans, like high-technology products. For products or services with a long life, like hotel safe deposit boxes, the acceptable payback period might be much longer because it is fairly predictable and secure.

PAYBACK PERIOD ASSESSMENT

One year or less	Great
Two years	Good
Three years	Passable
More than three years	A tough sell

Discovering Your Benefits

How does one go about identifying the best benefits for a product or service? By understanding it from the customer's viewpoint. The closer you can come to the customer's perspective, the better chance you have of identifying meaningful benefits. The best way to understand the customer's perspective, of course, is to talk to potential or real customers. Here are some suggestions for identifying key benefits:

The most important benefits from the customer's viewpoint may be those you haven't thought of or didn't consider important. In my own business, which includes producing newsletters for professional service firms, I recall being told by a client how the newsletter I produced made all the employees feel good about the firm. They liked seeing one another's names and photos in the newsletter and appreciated the favorable comments from clients about the publication.

• Be on the lookout for new benefits.

For me, that observation was a revelation. I had always thought of the newsletter in terms of how it helped my customer bring in new clients or encouraged existing clients to seek additional services. The fact that the newsletter helped improve employee morale was an emotional benefit. Clearly, then, you must constantly look for new benefits.

Identifying a number of small benefits can sometimes lead you to identify a large class of benefits. For Anita Roddick, observing many seemingly small irritations about

• Be alert to patterns.

the established cosmetics industry led her to see the larger benefit she could offer: an alternative cosmetics business.

• Be prepared to make assumptions.

In the case of financial benefits, you must be prepared to make some realistic assumptions or estimates. In the MicroFridge Profit Analysis shown on page 108, a list of assumptions is made about the number of appliances purchased, the room occupancy rates, the actual surcharge, and the number of customers per day buying food.

Or take interior designers for business, who promote their services based on increasing a company's revenues via improved productivity or that offer access to discounted furnishings. The actual amount of productivity improvement may vary from company to company in a range of, say, 7% to 10%. In promoting the company's services, then, the designer should settle on a percentage somewhere at the midpoint of the range.

Identifying benefits is in many instances a matter of ongoing research about your market. The next chapter is devoted to guiding you through the research essential to understanding your market.

The Knowledge-Information Factor

The benefits that are most important to your customers today may not be those that matter tomorrow. Executives who expect to keep their companies growing must build in techniques and approaches for keeping tabs of changing customer needs and desires. The best way to keep informed is through an ongoing stream of knowledge and information. Companies that develop systems for continually monitoring the marketplace and collecting and analyzing data on their customers are the ones that succeed over the long term. These companies are able to adjust their strategies to take account of fast-shifting market forces. Among the questions you should consider are the following:

- How will the information be collected?
- How will it be transmitted and shared through the organization?
- How will information be used to adjust the company's marketing approach?

The availability of low-cost computers makes it easier for companies to access and tabulate essential data. To make best use of such data, companies must establish databases, sales follow-up systems, and other such programs that allow data to be easily entered and analyzed. Thus, mail-order firms with appropriate systems can immediately access past buying records of customers who call in orders, determine the availability of products, make the charges, and initiate the packing and shipping—all with a few keystroke taps on the computer. Then, when it comes time to evaluate the company's marketing strategy, the information about where customers come from as well as their preferences and order patterns can be easily assembled.

The key to making information and knowledge effective elements of your marketing strategy lies in developing a company-wide approach to gathering, sharing, and using data. For example, salespeople are often privy to extremely valuable intelligence about customer tastes, changing needs, and competitor activities. Unless such information is actually written down and made available to others in the organization, though, it has no value beyond what the salesperson extracts.

The process of gathering such information needs to be standardized as much as possible. That is, employees should all be asking the same questions of customer prospects, existing customers, and others from whom information is being gathered. Direct-mail pieces and 800-number extensions should be coded so that data are systematically categorized. Among the techniques that should be considered are the following:

• Monitor inquiries.
Names, addresses, and phone numbers of anyone who inquires about company products and services should be gathered. In addition, customer prospects may be questioned about how they learned of the company's offerings, what additional information they require, and when they might make a decision about purchasing.

• Gather point-of-sale data.
This information includes the actual products or services being purchased along with as much data as possible about the individuals making the purchase. Supermarkets and other large retailers that rely on bar codes have turned such data gathering into a science. They can determine which products are bought at what time and, when credit cards are used, the age, sex, and home addresses of customers.

• Stay in contact with customers.
Find ways to follow up continually with customers about how they are using your products or services. This can take the form of telephone inquiries, questionnaires, or newsletters that include comment forms. What do users like and dislike about your product? What suggestions do they have for improvement?

Information about market studies and trends should be assembled on a regular basis. Similarly, competitor actions should be monitored. These tasks can be accomplished fairly easily by regularly using computerized databases. Industry names can be entered into databases that include newsletters, business magazines, and other business publications. Similarly, it is possible to obtain articles that describe competitor activities, as well as credit information from services like Dun & Bradstreet.

• Gather marketing intelligence.

Instead of being defensive about customer complaints, learn from them. Determine exactly what is upsetting customers—the frustration of not getting a straight answer, the unavailability of a product, the lack of attention to product detail, or whatever. Once again, all customers who complain should be asked the same questions.

• Learn from customer complaints.

Instituting such a company-wide systematic approach to gathering essential marketing data is no easy task. Here are two areas to pay special attention to in establishing your company's system:

Employees need to understand what is expected of them in gathering information. They need to know not only what questions to ask but when and how to ask them. For example, they should know what questions to ask before a sale and after the sale is completed. And different employees will have different questions; salespeople will not ask the same questions as repair people.

• Train employees to question prospects and customers.

• Build in systems for follow-up.

How are you going to follow up with customers after the sale or completion of warranty/repair work? Will you send out a questionnaire? What will it cover? How long will it be? Will you do telephone follow-up of those who don't answer the questionnaire? Or will you begin with a telephone inquiry?

Deciding on and establishing your systems at the time you develop your marketing strategy will go a long way toward ensuring effective implementation of a sound long-range marketing plan.

► **Exercises**

1. Describe in 25 words or less each of the four most important benefits
    your company's product or service provides. (Repeat the exercise for
    each of your company's additional products or services.)

2. Prioritize these benefits.

3. Label each benefit according to whether it is an emotional or a financial
    benefit.

4. For each financial benefit, calculate the financial savings or gain to
    the customer. Can you determine a payback period for your product or
    service? What is it? If it is longer than you want, can you think of ways
    to shorten it?

5. Describe three ways in which you will provide for the ongoing collection
    of knowledge and information to ensure you make appropriate adjust-
    ments of your marketing strategy.

6. How will the collection process be systematized in your company?

(Worksheets for this chapter are provided on page 282)

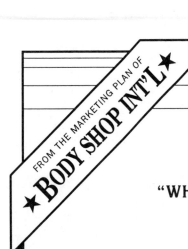

EXHIBIT 5-1

"WHAT IS THE BODY SHOP?"

The Body Shop is. . .
skin
and hair
and colour
and care
and commitment
and choice
and facts
and fun
and against animal testing
and. . .
all over the world

(from a Body Shop Brochure)

EXHIBIT 5–2

FROM THE MARKETING PLAN OF ★ MICROFRIDGE ★

HOTEL/MOTEL
PURCHASE JUSTIFICATION

Benefits

The major benefits of implementing this marketing plan are highlighted below:

Customer satisfaction and increased occupancy rates

The goal of the lodging industry is to maintain as high an occupancy rate as possible. As competition increases, in-room amenities become extremely important. Repeat customers are extremely likely as a result of the MicroFridge® use.

Increased revenues

The profit analysis shown above indicates that an investment of approximately $12,000 can yield a profit of about $158,000 over seven years. This is over a 1,000% return on investment! Even if food sales were not included, a profit in excess of $94,000 can be generated from a slight ($3) room surcharge. This is very conservative, since some properties are charging between $5-$7 per day with full occupancy in these rooms!

Significant revenues from food sales

Most properties have snack food vending machines where they receive 10% of food product sales. This plan enables the hotel/motel to generate and retain significant profits through the sale of meals and snacks which are inherently more attractive to customers than typical vending machine products.

5

Marketing Strategy

EXHIBIT 5–2
continued

No capital outlay using leasing plan and positive cash flow from month one!

Using the leasing plan presented above there is no initial expenditure and cash flow is positive from the first month on. The per unit monthly lease is about $12. At $3 per night, only 4 nights of the month would have to be occupied to break even. At 60% occupancy, revenues of $54 would be generated at a profit of $42 per month for each MicroFridge® unit.

Minimal labor contribution

It is anticipated that minimal additional labor contribution is necessary since outside food vendors are stocking the freezer and minimal additional maid time is needed to clean the room. Most microwavable products are now packaged in cook and serve containers and are therefore throw away items. MicroFridge® cleaning consists of "wiping down" the unit as is done for other in-room furniture.

Front desk time may increase minimally due to increased cash transactions. It is not anticipated, however, that this will require an increase in staff since most purchases will be made in bulk form (rather than repeated trips) or only at specific meal times (breakfast and late evening).

Competes with all-suite properties

The combination of food sales and an in-room "mini-kitchen" presents a highly competitive option to all-suite properties at a lesser cost.

EXHIBIT 5-2
continued

MICROFRIDGE

No wiring upgrades

Since most guest rooms are wired with 15 or 20 amp circuits, the existing wiring will be overloaded by the installation of a separate compact refrigerator and microwave oven combined with lighting, TV, hair dryer, etc. Due to the patented design of the MicroFridge®, no changes in circuitry are necessary.

In-room freezer

The MicroFridge® multipliance is the only product of its kind that combines three items into one and offers a fully functional freezer capable of storing frozen ice cubes.

Conclusions

MicroFridge Inc. presents an opportunity for the hotel/motel owner with limited or no food service to expand food service. It also gives the economy lodging owner the opportunity to compete with the all-suite industry. Most importantly, significant profits from room surcharges and food sales can be generated while at the same time increasing customer satisfaction and occupancies.

5

Marketing Strategy

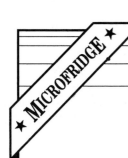

EXHIBIT 5-2
continued

PROFIT ANALYSIS

For the purpose of this simplified analysis, the following equipment and assumptions have been used:

• 25 MicroFridge® multipliances have been installed in guest rooms. Purchase price is $400 per unit. Total = $10,000.	• Five year leasing cost based on actual figures effective in February, 1990 and total amount financed is $12,050.
• Shipping expenses of $30 per unit have been built into the lease. Total = $750.	• $1 purchase option included.
	• Only 7 years of 10 year useful life included.
• State taxes of 5% have been built into the lease. Total = $500 (if applicable).	• 60% occupancy in rooms with MicroFridge® multipliances.
	• $3 per day surcharge.
• 21 cu. ft. freezer purchase price is $800 including shipping and taxes.	• $20 per year service allowance per unit.
• No advance lease payments are necessary.	• 50% mark-up on food sales.
	• 15 customers per day (60% X 25) buy an average of $5 worth of food per day.

EXHIBIT 5–2
continued

MICROFRIDGE

EQUIPMENT FINANCING SUMMARY

YEAR	LEASE	SERVICE ALLOWANCE	TOTAL REVENUE	NET PROFIT
1	3440	500	16,425	12,485
2	3440	500	16,425	12,485
3	3440	500	16,425	12,485
4	3440	500	16,425	12,485
5	3440	500	16,425	12,459
6		500	16,425	15,925
7		500	16,425	15,925
TOTAL	17,200	3,500	114,975	94,249

FOOD SALES

Daily food sales		
(15 customers/day X $5 each)	$	75.00
Less cost of food		(50.00)
Daily profit on food sales		25.00
Annualized (25 X 365)		9,125.00
Projected over 7 years		63,875.00

TOTAL PROFIT

MicroFridge® surcharge	$ 94,000.00
Food sales	64,000.00
Total profit	158,000.00
Total profit per MicroFridge® unit	**$ 6,320.00**

Marketing Strategy

5

EXHIBIT 5-2

continued

LETTER FROM A MICROFRIDGE CUSTOMER

FROM THE MANAGER OF A NATIONAL HOTEL CHAIN OUTLET

Bob Bennett
c/o MicroFridge
1 Merchant St.
Sharon, MA 02067

Dear Bob:

Over the past seven months I have purchased twenty MicroFridge units from your company. I thought that your company would be interested in a performance report from a hotel on your product.

Over the years, I have heard guests requests rooms with a kitchenette or an efficiency. The cost and insurance prohibit this in almost all hotels. The MicroFridge has replaced this demand for my hotel. The guest can now store soft drinks, beer, milk, and juices. Also, cold cuts, condiments, and many more food items.

The microwave is cost efficient for the guests. Now they can reheat pizzas, sandwiches, leftover dinners, or just heat up a number of frozen dinners from any grocery store.

These units are a great amenity for the long-term guest. Most of our long-term guests are on a per-diem or on a budget. It saves guests lots of money and time when they can prepare a quick sandwich or heat up a frozen dinner in a few minutes. It makes a great difference when you can buy a six-pack of beer for $3 in the grocery store to put in your MicroFridge. This saves a lot of time and money rather than having to leave your room every hour or so to buy a beer in the bar or lounge for approximately $1.75 each.

The twenty units have paid for themselves in the past six months. Our hotel rents the units out for $7 per day. We had 18 units rented out for 64 days straight. It takes only 58 days of rental for the MicroFridge to pay for itself.

We now have reservations requesting, "Please put a MicroFridge in my room."

In closing, the MicroFridge has become a great amenity for my hotel rooms. It helps the guest in many ways and has increased my revenue.

Thanks for a great unit.

(The hotel manager)

YOUR PLACE IN THE MARKET

How Do Customers Perceive You?

T im DeMello couldn't have asked for more favorable conditions in which to launch his first Wall Street product back in 1987. When the stock market crashed in October, his company's $99 game—a stock guide, $100,000 of pretend money, and a toll-free number customers call to buy and sell shares—got lots of publicity in *The Wall Street Journal* and on "The Today Show." The company's phones rang off the hooks with inquiries and still more press coverage.

Unfortunately, the game's initial sales failed to dazzle most of the toy retailers who stocked it. Even when Brookstone, the powerful direct-mail seller of offbeat tools and games, began promoting the game in its catalogs, in

1988, results were disappointing. "On a scale of one to ten, it was a three," recalls DeMello.

In late 1988 DeMello convinced AT&T to sponsor the game as a four-month contest among college students, known as the AT&T Collegiate Investment Challenge. "That fall we sold about $500,000 worth of product," recalls DeMello—much more in three months than the company had sold the previous year. "When that happened, I said, 'I think we have something.' "

What was really going on here? Obviously, having AT&T behind the product was helpful, but DeMello had Brookstone's support and impressive national publicity with nowhere near the sales he achieved with the Collegiate Investment Challenge.

Two fundamental changes had occurred in the fledgling company's marketing strategy. First, the company moved from targeting upscale professionals and college professors to college students. "On campuses, new customer turnover is 25% a year, and word-of-mouth advertising is very cheap," says DeMello. "There are 7,000 colleges and some 12 million students, 30% of whom take business courses."

Second, the company changed the product's place, or position, in the market. "We had been positioning the company as a game company," recalls DeMello. "But when we were able to get the AT&T sponsorship, I realized we were really in the event business."

With those two changes, Wall Street Games' sales took off. But the struggle it went through to find the right "marketing formula," as it were, illustrates two key strategic issues facing many companies: targeting and positioning. Those are the subjects that must be understood to write the section of the marketing plan on market position.

Targeting the Right Market

Who are your customer prospects? Which among them are your *best* prospects?

These may seem like very basic questions to be asking at this point. Everyone knows who they are trying to sell to. And executives quickly learn to distinguish between promising and unpromising prospects.

But what you see often isn't what you get. Executives may find their answers to these questions are incorrect (if they are lucky enough to make the discovery), because they failed to appreciate the importance of three basic marketing principles:

The people or organizations that you think are your customer prospects may not be your ultimate customer prospects. This is especially likely if your prospects are not the final consumers—if you sell to other businesses or organizations instead of directly to the public.

1. Primary vs. derived demand.

Take the case of MicroFridge. The purchaser of the company's combination microwave oven-refrigerator-freezer on college campuses is typically the director of housing. So founder Bob Bennett spent much of the company's first year (1989) trying to convince them to order the product for dormitories. "We hit safety a lot," recalls Bennett. "Get rid of the hot plates that students are bringing in against the rules."

The approach wasn't very successful. "The housing directors know about the safety problem, but they don't want to be reminded of it. It's a negative."

Then Bennett struck on an idea. Why not have the housing directors survey their students about the desirability of having a MicroFridge? "We had to find the entrepreneurial ones willing to do the survey," says Bennett. Needless to say, the majority of students surveyed thought the MicroFridge was a great idea, even at a rental cost of $50 yearly.

Indeed, the surveys went so well that Bennett stopped trying to convince housing directors to do the surveys and offered to have MicroFridge do them. "Now the housing directors just have to check off a box to get us in to do the survey. We'll set up at the student union."

The lesson is clear to Bob Bennett: "Ultimately, our customer is the student. But the students will never even see the MicroFridge unit unless the housing director gets it to them."

A persuasive way to sell a product or service to a buyer who isn't the end-user is to provide evidence that the end-user wants it. With that evidence in hand, Bennett can move on to his main sales pitch: "There are all kinds of selling points for our product, but the main sales point is retention—keep students in the dorm."

Bennett's discovery was of the difference between primary and derived demand. Because he was selling to individuals who weren't actually the end-users, his market was based on derived demand—the perception of need by someone removed from the actual user. When he surveyed the students, he measured primary demand—the interest in the product by the final user.

Businesses that sell their products or services to other businesses—to retailers, distributors, wholesalers, or major corporations—are often selling based on derived demand. In many respects, selling directly to the end-user and responding to primary demand, as The Body Shop, Syms, and CareerTrack do, is less complicated. As long as the executives running these businesses stay attuned to what their customers want, the businesses can adjust to changes in primary demand.

Selling based on derived demand becomes complicated when the company's immediate customers are reacting to issues other than primary demand. Smartfoods discovered such complications when it sought to get its cheddar cheese popcorn onto supermarket chain shelves.

Here is how Ken Meyers describes Smartfoods' early attempts to get into supermarket chains: "Our efforts to get into the major chains were like anybody's—it is a long, slow, arduous process where you are pushing water uphill. And we were coming in during the early days of slotting allowances [a system of fees charged to manufacturers by supermarkets to get displayed on grocery shelves]. What really contributed to our distribution growth and success was backing the chains into taking on our product as a function of pent-up consumer demand."

The consumer demand emanated from main two sources, says Meyers: the company's presence in convenience stores and its aggressive efforts to distribute product samples at road races, ski areas, and beaches. "A per-

6

Your Place in the Market

fect example of this was how we got in Price Chopper, in upstate New York. We weren't ready for upstate New York yet, but Price Chopper called us up and said, 'Hey, come on out and see us. You guys make a product that some of our consumers are beating us on the head for.' Consumers had been exposed to the product one way or another. They would go to the managers of these stores and say, 'Do you have Smartfood? I want Smartfood. Why don't you get it?' The managers listened to just so much of this and they would call their buyers and say, 'Listen, go get this product. I am sick and tired of this.' So we jumped into upstate New York a little faster than we had expected to."

Because the matters of primary and derived demand are so key to MicroFridge's ultimate success, they are a central element of the company's marketing plan (see Exhibit 6–1, page 128). As the marketing plan makes clear, there is more to affecting derived demand than demonstrating the existence of primary demand.

A connection needs to be made between primary and derived demand so a company's immediate customer realizes the benefits of catering to primary demand. Thus, the MicroFridge marketing plan notes the necessity to, "Elicit commitment from Housing to accommodate student demand." The plan points out the necessity of providing housing directors with "success stories"—cases of colleges improving their retention rates of students in the dormitories and of the increased profitability that comes with such improvement.

In its marketing plan, MicroFridge also includes a sample of a "Purchase Justification" document for housing directors. The document is similar to the one MicroFridge distributes to hotel/motel managers (described in Chapter 3), hammering home the evidence of primary demand (see Exhibit 6–2, page 129). Note that the first four advantages are outgrowths of primary demand. In describing them,

Price as a Positioning Tool

What is the role of price in positioning products and services?

A perusal of your daily newspaper or junk mail illustrates how pervasive are companies' attempts to position their products and services as having the most attractive prices.

Just because price is widely used doesn't make it the most effective positioning tool, however. Part of the reason it is used so often is that it is easy to communicate. Competitive pressures, discussed in detail in the next chapter, are another force at work.

For many companies, the problem with price as a positioning tool is that they get caught up in price wars that erode profits and can be won only by those with the deepest pockets. Any number of appliance, clothing, and furniture stores have gone out of business because they couldn't sustain the price wars.

If used properly, though, pricing can be one part of effective positioning. For instance, Syms has become known for marking its products down by a set percentage every ten days. According to Marcy Syms, "We are in effect telling consumers that as merchandise ages, it loses its value to the retailer." That approach fits in with the company's overall position as the retailer of choice for the "educated consumer."

MicroFridge plays on such emotions as fear and greed. The absence of such conveniences as microwaves and freezers in student housing often leads "to student dissatisfaction and often times a search for alternative housing, since it provides more independence," the justification notes.

2. Your market segment.

In Chapter 4, I discussed segmentation in broad industry terms. But the issue of segmentation—grouping or categorizing customer prospects—usually becomes more complicated once you have determined you are targeting a particular part of an industry, such as the soft-cookie segment that R.W. Frookies initially went after.

Besides an industry segment, markets can be segmented further based on geography, demographics, and buyer tastes or experience. Both R.W. Frookies and Smartfoods initially segmented their markets beyond the soft-cookie or snack-food segments. Both sought to establish themselves in the Northeast before going after other areas of the country. Both also targeted health-conscious consumers.

One common means of segmentation is to differentiate between experienced and inexperienced buyers. Generally, experienced buyers are preferable to inexperienced ones because the latter require that you educate them about many issues.

But segmentation can cut a lot of different ways, some of them counterintuitive. Bob Bennett of MicroFridge initially went after college housing directors of all types, but soon found that college housing offices broke down into two segments. "There were those that allow microwaves and those that don't," he recalls. The housing directors within each segment differ widely in personality and business style, he discovered. "Those that allow microwaves are more entrepreneurial and risk-taking. The students have talked the director into allowing microwaves."

Those that didn't allow microwaves tended to be more conservative. "These housing directors turned out to be our best customers," he says. "They were more likely to let me make my case." Because the dorms didn't have any microwaves, "There was no existing competition to flush out. There was also more likely a bigger student-retention problem, because the housing people were not satisfying what has come to be conventional student demand."

For Syms, the segmentation occurs among likely buyers of discount clothing. "It's an upscale audience," says David Bernard, director of advertising. "It's the kind of person who watches 'Jeopardy' as opposed to 'Wheel of Fortune.' Our customers are major users of clothing. They have an interest in brand names."

Such characteristics distinguish the Syms customer from the K mart one, in Bernard's view. "We don't sell cheap clothes. We sell brand-name clothes at far below cost. That can work against us. If you are looking for cheap and you don't find it, you will tell your friends that Syms is too expensive. It is very important that our advertising delivers the right person into the store."

6

Your Place in the Market

As MicroFridge and Syms's marketing efforts make clear, you can waste resources pursuing prospective customers who aren't in the right segment for your company's products or services. Conversely, the sales effort becomes much easier once you have identified the appropriate segment. MicroFridge salespeople can call college housing offices and begin with a simple question: Do you allow microwaves in your dorms? If the answer is no, the sales pitch can begin. If the answer is yes, the salesperson can move on to the next prospect. No need to schedule meetings, forward printed material, and do all the other things that cost time and money.

Finally, it should be noted that segments can be very narrow and specific. Very small slices of larger markets are often referred to as "niche markets." Industry newsletters can get very highly focused, for example, addressed to the maintenance engineers of electric power plants or to marketing executives of gas companies. Catering to a narrow niche may limit growth but allow for higher prices because of the specialization required.

3. Your position in the market.

The key question here is, How do customers perceive your company and its product or service? Are you viewed as a provider of premium products whose high quality justifies a top price? Or are you considered a maker of adequate-quality products made attractive by their below-average prices?

Of course, the matter of positioning is related to segmentation. Once you know the segment you are going after, you can position yourself to be attractive to that segment. Thus, Syms's motto, "An educated consumer is our

Staying in Touch with Customers

Every company, no matter what its size, must establish approaches for monitoring customer needs. There are two basic ways to stay in touch with customers:

• *Anecdotal feedback.* The term anecdotal refers to the fact that feedback you get in individual or small-group conversations with prospects and customers isn't scientific. Anecdotal feedback can come from anyone who has contact with prospects and customers—most typically salespeople and executives. This feedback should be formalized as much as possible—for example, by having salespeople fill out forms recording reactions from failed prospects. Another, more formal approach is to use focus groups consisting of six to eight individuals representing the target market, who are questioned by a trained facilitator. Their reactions can be observed by executives and even recorded for later study.

• *Surveys.* This is a more scientific approach that requires putting together a questionnaire to sample a large number of prospects and/or customers. Answers to the questionnaire are typically obtained by telephone or through the mail. Sometimes, though, results can be gathered by including the questionnaire in a company newsletter or by having researchers on site at a store or shopping mall.

The more responses obtained, the more reliable the results will be. Several hundred responses from a diverse group of prospects and/or customers usually provide significant insights.

Two keys to success: Formulate the questions carefully so you are addressing key marketing issues, and keep the questions and the questionnaire as simple and to the point as possible.

6

Your Place in the Market

best customer," is an effort to appeal to upscale consumers likely to value education. The company builds on that theme by providing information about its buying and markdown practices that an educated individual may be interested in.

A company's position will likely change over time. Ideally, this change is based on customer feedback. Wall Street Games changed its position by breaking its target market into two segments—a professional and nonprofessional segment (see Exhibit 6–3, page 131). "We received hundreds of unsolicited comments recommending PRO and NON-PRO Divisions," notes the plan. Many of those comments were from customers who felt they were up against stock market experts who would inevitably perform best. As the plan notes, many customers were "disenchanted by the perception that they would never win because they are pitted against professionals. The conclusion is that while the prizes themselves may not be important, participant's ability to break into the top ten is important."

By satisfying the complaints, company executives reasoned, they would be able to return to past customers and prospects with a new position, and proposition: The game is now fairer and thus more fun. Come on back. As Tim DeMello puts it, "The only reason this company has made it is this company has been adaptable."

Pathways to the Best Position

Achieving the identity that serves your company most effectively in the marketplace stems from a keen understanding of the marketplace and its needs. You must understand the market in terms of its size and trends, as well as its tastes and desires.

I am talking here about the kind of understanding that is rarely available from articles and studies about your industry. It usually comes from your personal observations and interactions with customers and prospects.

All the talk about staying "close to the customer" relates to your identity in the market. You must understand what the market wants before you can properly establish your position.

You also need to apply correctly the lessons you learn from the marketplace. Unless you have a monopoly position in the market, like an electric utility or cable-television station, you will be unable to push the market to take something it doesn't want. You must be prepared to adjust your product or service to match the needs of prospective and longtime customers.

Here are some approaches for achieving the best position:

Determining what customers are doing is usually the easy part—which you can learn from reading trade publications, talking with industry analysts, and observing consumers at shopping malls. It is much more difficult to understand why they are moving in certain directions.

• Learn the whats and whys.

Wall Street Games knew it wasn't getting the kind of repeat business from customers it thought it should get. It took longer to determine why more people weren't playing the game again. The realization that some customers were

6

Your Place in the Market

turned off by the perceived influence of professional investors made the company's change in positioning a sensible one.

• Distinguish between needs of immediate and ultimate customers.

When your immediate customers aren't your ultimate ones, you can become preoccupied with servicing the former—to the detriment of the latter. MicroFridge learned that lesson when it tried to meet the concerns of housing directors.

Companies that remain preoccupied with catering to derived demand will encounter difficulties if that demand is based on needs different from primary demand—as it invariably is. The immediate customer needs to respond to primary demand or face problems. Housing directors who ignored student demand for the convenience afforded by microwave ovens and refrigerators risked losing student tenants and being stuck with empty rooms. As much as the housing officials may personally dislike the appliances (along with other inducements to make students happy), they need to make them available to students.

• Determine why prospects are not buying.

Most people are uncomfortable telling a seller the real reasons they don't like what is being sold. So they make up reasons—they don't have the budget or the time or they'll think about it.

But invariably more substantial issues are involved. Sometimes you can find out by engaging the prospects in nonthreatening ways—for instance, inquiring what the ideal product or service of the type you are selling would include and what benefits it would provide.

Sometimes, though, the prospective customers may not even be able to articulate their reasons for rejections, as Bob Bennett of MicroFridge found out. So you need more than feedback. You need to think in terms of the fundamentals discussed previously—industry trends, customer benefits, primary demand, and segmentation—and come up with approaches for getting your answers. Bennett came up with the device of polling students to help him make the ultimate determination of who his best prospects were and how to convince them to buy.

Changing your position in the market isn't something that should be done lightly, as it is fraught with risk. If you have a going business and are at least moderately profitable, you run the risk that you will turn off your longtime customers. For example, if Syms suddenly decided it needed to draw prospective customers looking for "cheap" clothing, it could alienate its upscale customer base.

Another potential pitfall is that the new position may not work. To take the Syms case a step further, the company may wind up not attracting the "cheap" crowd in the numbers anticipated. In that scenario, it would wind up with the worst of both worlds—alienating both segments and losing a reliable customer base.

One way around such a situation is to experiment with a position change before rolling it out full scale. In the Syms case, the company might try a position change in one or two stores, or one geographic area, before going national. That way, it can collect reactions and data to decide whether to proceed.

Clearly, the matters of segments and positioning are fundamental to any marketing strategy. They are also typically subtle and complex, requiring much thought and analysis. Executives need to probe and assess their positions to find the right formula. (And even then, it may not remain the right formula for long.)

▶ Exercises

1. Are your company's sales a result of primary or derived demand?

2. If sales stem from derived demand, list at least three benefits your company's products and/or services offer to end-users.

3. How do you communicate the importance of those benefits to your immediate customers?

4. Describe your company's precise segment of the market.

5. Indicate your company's position in its segment.

6. Explain how price fits into your company's positioning approach.

7. Describe at least two approaches you have planned over the next year for monitoring customer/prospect attitudes.

6

Your Place in the Market

(Worksheets for this chapter are provided on page 285)

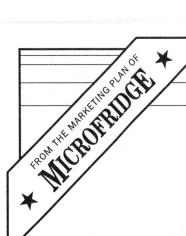

EXHIBIT 6–1

FROM THE MARKETING PLAN OF ★ MICROFRIDGE ★

MARKETING PLAN

- Survey students on cooking, desire for product, willingness to pay more in board and willingness to stay on campus if they have MF convenience.

- Elicit commitment from Housing to accommodate student demand.

- Direct mailing in January to 751 Housing Directors explaining success stories.

- Offer free 90-day evaluation to support surveys.

- Build application note on U. Pitt, Johnstown program and circulate.

- Develop new college brochure and distribute.

- Develop network of student reps. to survey and help sell.

EXHIBIT 6–2

FROM THE MARKETING PLAN OF
★ *MICROFRIDGE* ★

MICROFRIDGE MULTIPLIANCE
COLLEGE/UNIVERSITY
PURCHASE JUSTIFICATION

ADVANTAGES

1. Improved quality of life

Today's students have grown up with and are accustomed to a refrigerator, freezer and microwave oven. When they get to college, these conveniences are many times restricted, leading to student dissatisfaction and often times a search for alternative housing since it provides more independence. Housing sells convenience. The MicroFridge® multipliance is convenience that improves quality of life and fosters the independence that students desire. Students love the product. Providing it campus-wide will be viewed as a tremendous improvement in residence hall life and will allow preparation of evening snacks and hot drinks.

2. Improved retention

Providing additional convenience should lead to higher retention of upperclass students.

3. Minimal cost to students

An annual fee of $50 per student for this type of in-room amenity is extremely inexpensive. The common sales price is over $400 and the common annual rental cost is $150 plus a damage deposit. A survey of students should verify the demand and acceptance of the annual fee. A sample survey is attached.

6

Your Place in the Market

EXHIBIT 6-2

continued

★ MICROFRIDGE ★

4. Profit generation

If the college desires to make residence halls profit centers rather than cost center, the $156 and $448 per unit profit contributions are significant.

5. Reduced liability exposure

MicroFridge Inc. has conducted independent surveys at a number of colleges which conclude that approximately 90% of students are cooking with prohibited appliances—primarily hot plates, toaster ovens and microwave ovens. Installing a safe MicroFridge® multipliance in each room eliminates the need for these other items and, therefore, reduces the legal liability from fire. The National Fire Protection Association reported that there were 2,500 reported fires per year in all residence halls during the period of 1983 through 1987.

6. Food service profits

Profits can also be generated by selling selected frozen and microwavable food products (popcorn, pizza, ice cream, etc.) through the bookstore or a convenience store.

EXHIBIT 6-3

FROM THE MARKETING PLAN OF
★WALL STREET GAMES★

1ST QUARTER 1992 MARKETING PLAN
NATIONAL INVESTMENT CHALLENGE
WALL STREET GAMES

The plan for the NIC 1st Quarter 1992 is to deliver $137,000 of contribution to overhead. We plan on attaining 6,200 participants by spending $160,000 ($25 acquisition cost).

The main course of action has been to reposition the National Investment Challenge with a PRO and NON-PRO Division which is devised to bring back the past customers (30,000) and ignite past inquiries (50,000) that are currently in the database. To strengthen this repositioning a second first class mailing, in addition to the third class database mailing, will be targeted at the most recent past customers and inquiries. By initiating this first class mailing our best prospects will have a quicker and more frequent look at our new competition. This will also complement an early and intense planned broker calling effort. This double mailing and intense broker calling effort should justify the increased sales numbers in the database category. In addition, we also hope to retain more current participants and increase referral conversion through a more personal inquiry letter.

The design and structure of the new competition has come directly from customer interaction and feedback (e.g. the two surveys recently done). We received hundreds of unsolicited comments recommending PRO and NON-PRO Divisions. In addition, the typical NIC customer is playing the competition for education, competition and strategy testing and not the prizes, although many are disenchanted by the perception that they would never win because they are pitted against professionals. The conclusion is that while the prizes themselves may not be important, participant's ability to break into the top ten is important.

Your Place in the Market

6

ASSESSING THE COMPETITION

How Do You Stack Up?

The terminology used to describe competition between businesses closely resembles that of warfare. Companies "battle" each other for market share. They "are locked in combat" and "fight it out" for customers. Each wants to "destroy" the other, and losers become "casualties."

The warlike language crops up for good reason: Competition is fierce and, in certain strategic respects, resembles warfare.

In their market planning, however, many executives fail to give the competition the attention it deserves. If there is one error of omission executives make more commonly than any other, it is that they fail to take the competition as seriously as they should.

That's because executives often become so enamored of their own product or service that they tend to minimize the competition. It's as if they feel their product or service is of such superior quality or has such an attractive price that there is simply no way prospective buyers would consider another option.

Of course, this isn't how the feeling is articulated. Rather, executives often say there isn't much competition because "no one does exactly what we do." Or they rationalize that they are more focused and harder driving than the competition.

Part of the problem is that executives just aren't sure how to deal with competition from a planning viewpoint. In U.S. society, we are taught to believe we can always beat the competition. Therefore, to take the competition too seriously is akin to admitting weakness.

But smart executives know that realistic planning requires understanding the competition as completely as possible. The reason has nothing to do with weakness, and everything to do with being successful.

In today's marketplace, you ignore the competition at your own peril. Just ask the executives of America's automobile, consumer electronics, steel, machine tool, and assorted other industries.

It doesn't matter whether you are in a start-up situation or well established in the marketplace. If you are just starting a business, you will find that established competitors are more protective of their markets than ever before. They will offer discounts, improve service, and do what's necessary to keep new companies from stealing their customers. And if you are already in business, you are likely seeing a parade of start-ups as well as established competitors trying to take market share from you, using ever more aggressive tactics.

In this chapter, I provide guidance for identifying, assessing, and learning more about the competition. One approach to assessing the competition involves consideration of three questions:

1. Who Is the Competition?

This is another simplistic question any self-respecting executive should be able to answer without hesitation. But in reality, many executives have difficulty with it, and for good reason: The answer often isn't obvious, and in most industries is getting less obvious as competitive lines blur.

For example, try identifying the competition of the *Harvard Business Review*. The magazine is unusual in that it is a business publication appealing to both academics and managers. There are other academic journals and business-management magazines, but none has achieved the special position of the *Harvard Business Review*.

When I was an editor with the publication, we struggled with the matter of identifying competition. Obviously, competition consisted of a few other university-sponsored business journals that had only a fraction of *HBR*'s subscription base and never achieved wide acceptance among middle- and senior-level managers. Competition also included other mass-circulation business magazines like *Fortune*, *Business Week*, and *Inc.*, which cover management issues.

But when we asked subscribers who didn't renew why they chose to drop the publication, the most frequent answer was that they didn't have the time to read *HBR*'s articles. That sounded innocuous enough, since the *Harvard Business Review* is substantive and requires a time investment.

But that answer also contained the seeds of competitive problems. All business executives have some extra time to keep abreast of important management developments. So when executives said they didn't have time, they were really saying they didn't have time for *us*. That meant they were using the time once devoted to *HBR* for some other resource for staying on top of important management developments—essentially, our nameless, faceless competition.

We came to the conclusion that we were in competition with not only other academic and mass-circulation business publications, but with all business-management sources such as business newspapers, videos, and seminars. In the final analysis, we were competing with all these for an executive's most precious commodity—his or her time. Unless we could make a convincing case that our publication was more valuable than these sources, we were going to lose out. Out of that understanding came efforts to shorten articles, provide executive summaries of articles, include more interesting graphics, and other techniques for packaging the product to appeal to increasingly time-sensitive readers.

Therefore, while the answer of who your competition is looks obvious, it is usually more involved than it first appears. If you have a hardware store, a restaurant, or a grocery store, the competition would seem to be the other hardware stores, restaurants, and supermarkets in your community. As many such businesses have discovered, however, competition comes from numerous sources.

For hardware stores, significant competition has come from the mass-market chains like Home Depot. Many restaurants have discovered their markets being eroded by supermarkets offering salad bars and takeout lunches and dinners. And supermarkets have in many cases lost business to such buying clubs as Costco and BJ's, which sell consumer electronics, meats, paper products, and canned goods.

Sometimes the competition comes from far-off companies using different distribution channels. Among the most serious competitors for many retailers are the mail-order firms. Such companies as L.L. Bean and Lands' End are increasingly important players in the clothing industry. Even such items as fresh flowers and wine are now available through mail order, which should make owners of florist and liquor stores more than a little nervous.

The competition comes from other countries as well. We all know about the competitive pressures placed on the U.S.'s auto, steel, textile, and electronics industries by overseas competitors. In recent years, global competitors have invaded ever narrower and seemingly mundane industries. Take the printing business. Printers in Asia have succeeded in attracting some U.S. companies that do large volumes of printing because Asia's low-cost labor can reduce printing bills substantially. U.S. restaurants are increasingly experiencing competition from chains based in Europe. Designer kitchen fixtures and other home furnishings from Europe have poured into the U.S. marketplace.

Now that I have demonstrated how wide ranging competition is, how can you make sense of the matter from a planning perspective? A useful approach is to separate your competition into three groups, from the most obvious to the least obvious competitors, as follows:

• **Direct, or segment, competition.**	These are the competitors that are not only in the same business as you, but are going after the same target market. Thus, direct competition to Syms isn't necessarily all clothing discounters, but those going after its upscale buyers who value designer labels at discount. One such competitor is the fast-growing Filene's Basement chain, which specializes in selling premium clothing at deep discount.

CareerTrack, in the section of its marketing plan on competition, indicates the difficulties associated with identifying direct competitors (see Exhibit 7–1, page 157). The main challenge is that "more than 6,000 companies in the U.S. engage in some aspect of seminar production," observes the plan. But CareerTrack's executives have concluded that many are not direct competitors because, "The |

majority of companies in the industry are small firms with a limited number of employees and limited annual revenues. Typically, these companies are consulting firms specializing in a particular industry or human resources problem. By contrast, CareerTrack is the largest company of its kind in the industry, with over 425 employees and over $66 million in annual revenue."

When all is said and done, CareerTrack identifies a handful of organizations "as its most direct competition." These direct competitors approach CareerTrack in size and in having a wide range of seminar topics.

However, an examination of the "Competitor Matrix" that is a part of the section on competition suggests that other factors are equally or more important. For instance, both the American Management Association (AMA) and Dale Carnegie are larger than CareerTrack in revenue and estimated number of programs. The four organizations identified, however, are much closer to CareerTrack in price, seminar length, and seminar size. For CareerTrack, then, the directness of competition may hinge more on such matters as price, seminar length, and seminar size than on company size or seminar topic range.

Fortunately for CareerTrack, though its descriptive material on the competition doesn't articulate the criteria very well, its executives have used appropriate criteria to identify direct competitors. The issue of criteria isn't just one of semantics, however. If faulty criteria are used to identify competitors, you may find yourself honing in on

7

Assessing the
Competition

the wrong guys. You will waste resources competing with companies that aren't direct competitors, and real competitors may do damage to you before you're aware of what is going on.

Which criteria should you use to identify direct competitors? The same criteria you used to determine your market segment and position. Those companies that target at least some of your segment and position themselves in ways similar to your company deserve consideration as potential direct, or segment, competition.

• Industry competition.

CareerTrack correctly concluded that while a handful of companies deserved being identified as direct competitors, many others warranted consideration as competitors because they were in the same industry. It is not enough to conclude that all those in your industry not identified as direct competitors are indirect competitors. In many industries, that would leave hundreds or even thousands of competitors. That is not specific enough to be of practical value.

Companies that qualify as industry competitors are those that do not primarily target your segment of the market, but target or serve some parts of it, have shown signs of doing so, or have the capacity to do so. CareerTrack recognizes the importance of being precise in identifying industry competitors. As the company's plan observes after identifying the four direct competitors, "In addition, there are several organizations that compete with CareerTrack as members of the training industry, although indirectly because of the products and services they offer (these competitors produce high-priced, multi-day seminars)."

In today's complex marketplace, this is often the most important source of future competition. Consider, for example, video rental stores' competition. Direct competition generally consists of other video rental stores in the same community. Industry competition might be video rental stores outside the community and cable movie channels and local or national television stations. But looking ahead, telephone companies are gaining the capacity to transmit television over telephone lines. When consumers can routinely push a few buttons on their telephone, television, or computer and watch first-run movies for $2 or $3, the competitive effects on video rental stores could be profound. Indeed, some of the large video chains began to respond to that threat in the early 1990s by putting great emphasis on selling videos as well as renting them.

In its plan CareerTrack identifies "approximately 100 to 150 colleges and universities that offer continuing education courses on professional development subjects." The schools are separate from the more than 6,000 companies providing seminars. They are usually operated as nonprofit organizations. But they have the capacity to attract individuals looking for the kind of low-cost self-improvement that CareerTrack offers. They thus qualify as indirect competition and deserve attention as competitors.

Other sources of competition to CareerTrack might be

• Indirect competition.

7

Assessing the Competition

139

self-improvement audio- and videotapes, the large number of self-help books that flooded the market in the late 1980s and 1990s, and the burgeoning numbers of career counselors and outplacement experts, some of whom offer seminars.

The difficulty of spotting indirect competition is that it can come from any of many different directions. The two best defenses against being caught off guard are, first, being open-minded about who might be classified as competition and, second, staying up-to-date through reading business and industry publications.

Too many executives get caught with blinders on when it comes to considering who might be competition, much as railroad executives did in the late nineteenth and early twentieth centuries when automobiles and airplanes were invented. The rail people thought they were competing against other railroads, when actually they were competing against all forms of transportation.

Taking the transportation example a step further, airline, car rental, and other transportation executives would be wise during the 1990s to stay abreast of such trends as video conferencing and computer networking, along with other approaches used to put groups of businesspeople into real-time contact with one another. As companies seek to cut travel expenses, such alternatives will become increasingly attractive, with an impact on air travel, auto rentals, hotels, and other such businesses. That means transportation executives should be reading publications reporting on computers, telecommunications, and related technologies.

2. What Do You Do About the Competition?

This is a question marketing experts debate endlessly. The reason the debate is never resolved is that no single suitable answer exists. Each executive must answer it based on the nature and seriousness of the competitive challenge at hand.

Certainly, competitive pressures of any sort are among the most severe any executive faces. There is a tendency to respond based on gut reactions. After all, you are in a form of warfare battling for survival, as I suggested at the beginning of this chapter. But because competitive issues are involved and complex, a more reasoned approach works best. Here are two matters to consider before going by your gut:

Are you in a growing or a stagnating market? Is it a new market or a mature market? The answers are important because they'll determine where you should focus your efforts in attracting customers. If you are in a growing market or a new market, then many of your prospective customers are likely not dealing with a direct or industry competitor. Your main challenge is to lure those prospects. To focus inordinate attention on taking customers from your competitors may distract you from your main priority, which is to win new customers before the competition does. On the other hand, if you are in a stagnating or mature market, your main source of new customers may be the disaffected customers of competitors. It may be wise, then, to concentrate on ways to win customers from competitors.

• The nature of your market.

• The price-cutting reflex.

Many executives' most immediate way of dealing with competitive pressures is to cut prices. And indeed, we regularly see price-cutting in such highly competitive industries as autos, consumer electronics, computers, and clothing. But is price-cutting really the best way to compete?

That depends on what you are selling, what your target market is, and what your position in the market is. In fields like computers, where fast-changing technology reduces the attractiveness of existing products, price-cutting may be entirely appropriate. In most cases, though, as we saw in the last chapter, attractive price will be only one component of your position in the marketplace.

As noted previously, Syms is an off-price retailer, but it doesn't pretend to have the lowest prices for all types of clothing. It specializes in providing consistently low prices on designer clothing. It may be that another chain will have a particular brand on a particular day at a lower price than Syms.

A more important challenge for Syms than matching other chains on price is to have the best possible selection of quality-brand clothing at discounted prices. Part of its competitive challenge is building and nurturing its relationships with clothing manufacturers and distributors so when attractive purchases become available, Syms officials will learn about them first and get good terms. "We never mention the names of manufacturers in our ads to protect them in their relationships" with department and specialty stores that charge full price, says Marcy Syms. To do otherwise would be to risk long-term relationships that underlie the company's success.

Even companies that successfully use price as part of their marketing strategy do so in an aggressive, innovative way rather than just reactively. CareerTrack's cofounder, Jimmy Calano, proudly asserts that the company "pioneered" the $99 all-day seminar in 1982 and, once again, the $45 all-day seminar in 1985. The key word here is *pioneered*. CareerTrack got prospective customers to sit up and take notice by aggressively lowering its price below that of competitors. One message to prospective customers was that this company works hard to provide them with value.

When competitors matched CareerTrack's $99 price, they didn't get the same marketplace credit. They were likely viewed as doing what they had to do, perhaps even showing signs of desperation. Moreover, they likely cut deeply into their own margins if they hadn't planned for the price cuts as CareerTrack had done, but were making them only because of CareerTrack's move. As CareerTrack's marketing section points out, "Although other companies have tried to compete with CareerTrack on price, they cannot match the Company's profitability at low prices, because they have not developed CareerTrack's sophisticated ancillary profit centers." These include audio- and videotapes, private seminars, and customer list rentals.

If you decide that competitive pressures demand a response, consider alternatives to price. Might you add ser-

• Stay focused.

143

vices? Improve convenience? Add distribution options? Or find a strategic partner?

Sometimes, the most creative approach is to keep doing what has made you successful and try to do it better. In this context, be sure not to underestimate the loyalty of the existing customer base for your product or service. When Smartfood was under competitive siege between 1986 and 1989, cofounder Ken Meyers was pleasantly surprised to discover that consumers weren't quick to drop his product for imitators, even at lower prices.

"We discovered that we had created a grand relationship," he recalls. "We weren't introducing people to a commodity. We were introducing people to a brand, which by its very nature instigates a relationship. Now, people either choose to preserve that relationship or they choose to cut it off. The one that we instigated was preserved by enough individuals that strength of our brand loyalty as was evidenced in New England was strong enough to stand the onslaught between 1986 and 1989 of the introduction of close to two dozen product introductions. Several of them were in black, green, and yellow bags, and two of them referred to Smartfood on the backs of their packages. One of them said, 'As good as Smartfood, but for half the price.' "

While Smartfood was able to withstand the competitive pressures in New England, Meyers concluded that the company couldn't roll the brand out nationally without additional artillery. By selling the company to Frito Lay in 1989, Smartfood could expand nationally without having to cut prices or otherwise significantly tamper with its success formula. And indeed, from 1989 to 1991, Smartfood annual sales under Frito Lay rose from $12.5 million to more than $50 million.

3. How Do You Stay Current with the Competition?

To avoid being surprised by the competition, you must know what it is up to. That is actually much easier to do than you might imagine, because an amazing amount of information about competitors is out there, waiting for you to exploit it. Here are two approaches for staying current with the competition:

1. Personal contact.

The best way to obtain information and insights about the competition is through personal observation. A 1992 article in *Inc.* illustrates how an aggressive entrepreneur, Tom Carns, decided to start a chain of very successful quick-printing shops in Las Vegas. He "went out and 'shopped' every quick-printing shop in Las Vegas—all 70 of them. He walked into each, looked around, and made copious mental notes. 'I watched how they treated their customers, what the business looked like, and how good the quality was,' Carns recalls."

Monitoring the competition in this way is easiest, of course, if you are in the retail business. But even if you aren't, there are other ways to do it.

Your sales representatives are in a position to learn a

7

Assessing the Competition

145

great deal about competitors because they are crossing paths with them to win customers. Your salespeople meet competitor salespeople in waiting rooms and in hotels. Most important, your salespeople are in regular contact with the best judges: customer prospects. Their assessments and reactions to competitors provide the most useful insights you can obtain.

But to gain the benefit of your salespeople's observations and experiences, you must find ways to mine the data. You must encourage them to write or record their discoveries. Provide simple forms or add the subject to prospect and order forms. Award prizes or bonuses to those who do the best job of providing competitive information. Include the providing of competitive information as a basis of job-performance evaluations.

Trade shows also provide valuable opportunities to rub shoulders with competitors. You can watch their new-product introductions and demonstrations as well as pick up their sales literature. Once again, you have the opportunity to quiz customer prospects about their reactions to competitor displays and announcements.

And don't automatically assume that competitors won't share information directly with you. Of course, if you are competing in a particular town or community, you shouldn't expect competitors to be forthcoming. But if your competition is geographically diverse, you might find competitors eager to share their insights and learn about yours. Industry trade gatherings can be excellent places to find out about new technology, customer trends, and other valuable market information.

The explosion of business publications and computerized databases makes it easy to gather valuable competitive information without ever leaving company headquarters. To keep abreast of the competition you can regularly scan databases of business, industry, and other publications for information on competitive companies.

2. Written sources.

You'll probably have an easier time gathering information about competitors that are publicly held because such companies are required by law to file regular reports with the Securities and Exchange Commission, and are open to public scrutiny. These reports often provide important information about product- or service-line performance, as well as executives' assessments of problems and opportunities. These reports are available in Washington, D.C., and at some university business school libraries. There are also several database and research companies that specialize in monitoring such filings.

But thanks to a variety of computerized databases, information about private companies has become more widely available. Articles in the business and local press stored in computerized databases often provide valuable tips and clues about competitors' activities. For example, articles may tip you off to lawsuits; these are available to the public and, in some cases, the written charges or responses provide surprising amounts of data about execu-

7

Assessing the Competition

tives' backgrounds, production processes, and company strategy. It is also possible to monitor patent applications, which provide important insights into research-and-development efforts and new products.

Don't assume that everything you learn through computerized sources is correct. One frequently used resource is credit reports tabulated by such companies as Dun & Bradstreet. These companies monitor private and public companies and gather credit and other financial data like revenues, assets, and number of employees.

The problem is that such data may be inaccurate simply because many private companies, in answering questions posed by the credit reporting companies, purposely understate or overstate the numbers to throw competitors off.

The challenge in maximizing the benefits of competitive data is to capture, store, and use it systematically. The key issue isn't getting enough information, but making use of what is available.

The explosion of data has led to the creation of a marketing discipline known as competitive intelligence. Specialists in competitive intelligence advise executives to develop systems and approaches for making sure data about competitors is properly collected, tabulated, and applied in market planning. That requires making competitive intelligence a high-priority company-wide matter.

As the quest for competitive data heats up, though, some executives use aggressive tactics to obtain it. These include hiring employees from competitors, questioning competitors' suppliers, and even sifting through the garbage of competitor executives. Some executives even hire academics to do surveys of competitors to gather essential data. These and other techniques bring companies to a fine ethical, as well as legal, line. My advice is to be careful. When in doubt, consult with an attorney. There is a lot of readily available data that can provide many of the answers you are seeking.

Lessons from Competitive Battlefields

How can you best apply what you've learned about competitors? By maintaining a balanced and realistic attitude about competitive matters in your market planning. Here are some ways to do that:

I strongly believe that the best approach to competition is to follow the old adage: Know thine enemy.

As disdainful as you may feel about your competitors, you will invariably be better off viewing them with an open mind. If you look closely at your competitors, you may discover a few things.

An excellent example of a company learning from its competition is provided in the marketing section of R.W. Frookies' plan (see Exhibit 7–2, page 163). The section on the competition examines each major direct or industry competitor and its approach to the marketplace.

Though the analysis becomes a justification for

• Learn from the competition.

Frookies to plow ahead with its concept, it is clear that the company learned important lessons from its survey. The examination of Barbara's Cookies is especially instructive. By determining that this competitor uses health-food ingredients, produces irregularly shaped cookies, and is marketed mostly in health-food stores, Frookies could confidently develop its own position. It planned to have a taste more "widely accepted by the mass market," "be larger (2 inches in diameter) and look more like a 'normal' cookie," and "be in the cookie section of the supermarket."

In examining Pride of the Farm, Frookies notes pluses and minuses. "The product is fairly good, but the packaging is primitive and clearly targeted to the 'health conscious.' Pride of the Farm is sold exclusively in natural food stores. The quick success of this product is a further indication of the pent-up demand for a healthy 'good for you' cookie."

• **Further develop your own strategy.**

A useful way to view the competitive battles is to ask yourself "what if" questions. What if your direct competitors suddenly reduce their prices significantly? What if a new competitor opens across the street from you? What if an indirect competitor becomes a direct competitor?

By asking such questions, you force yourself to consider more rationally, and in advance, your responses to competitive moves than if they occur as total surprises. The Frookies plan does this kind of "what if" planning in the section of its assessment that deals with Pepperidge Farm.

The plan observes, "Of all the current cookies producers, Frookies will be positioned similar to Pepperidge Farm. Like Pepperidge Farm, Frookies will offer several varieties of cookies around a common theme. The packaging for both companies (i.e., white backgrounds) is distinctive and attractive. Frookies will also be similar in terms of size and price point."

The obvious question is raised in the plan itself: "Could Pepperidge Farm develop a new line of products to compete with Frookies? Certainly. Nevertheless, there is a substantial record that shows that the first food product into the marketplace can retain its customer loyalty and expand its market in light of quality competition—as long as the product and approach to the market are good.

"It also would be difficult for Pepperidge Farm, or other major producers, to properly position a sugar-free cookie in relation to their current product lines. Currently, Pepperidge Farm is doing a growing and profitable business exclusively with sugar-based cookies. If the company came out with a new "healthy" sugar-free product, what would this say about its current line? Would Pepperidge Farm compete with itself and reduce the sales of its own cookies?"

By going through the "what if" exercise, Richard Worth has made a cogent case against one potential source of competition. He has some evidence to support his conclusion, as he notes his experience in a previous business, Sorrell Ridge jams, when Smucker's hesitated to respond competitively. Without asking the question, Worth might

7

Assessing the Competition

have worried unnecessarily about Pepperidge Farm at the expense of more legitimate competition expected to crop up from other sources.

If you fail to plan for competitive pressure, you risk falling into the gas-station-price-war mentality. When you do that, you may find yourself responding to other moves by competitors, rather than taking the initiative yourself. Essentially, you are letting the competition determine your marketing strategy.

I'm not suggesting that matching a price reduction by a competitor to hold onto market share is always inappropriate, because in certain situations you have no choice, such as when you want to hold onto an important customer. But I strongly suggest that when you take such an action, you also ask yourself what you can do to prevent it from happening again.

• Consider cooperation.

Just as in warfare, business competitors need not always be in conflict. In warfare, opposing countries have a way of seeking out alliances to advantage. Witness World War II, when fascist Germany allied with communist Russia for a brief time; after that alliance collapsed, capitalist United States allied with communist Russia for victory over Germany and Japan.

The old saying, My enemy's enemy is my friend, can apply in business. That helps explain how longtime archrivals Apple Computer and IBM could forge an alliance to develop products jointly. They decided the bigger enemy was Microsoft, so they were better off cooperating in certain areas than in continuing to beat each other down, possibly to Microsoft's advantage.

Many companies are looking to various forms of cooperation as an alternative to traditional competition. These cooperative arrangements, known by a variety of terms—strategic alliances, strategic partnerships, or joint ventures—can be an attractive alternative to traditional competitive battles. They are most appropriate when competitors complement each other's strengths and weaknesses; for example, if one company is especially strong in product development and a competitor stands out in distribution, the two can build on a strength and minimize weakness.

Improving productivity is one of the best ways to resist the temptation to cut prices. If you can produce the same product or service at a lower cost, you have room to not only reduce prices but to add features or benefits while keeping prices stable. And, in becoming more productive, companies are sometimes able to improve quality. Then they have the best of all worlds: lower costs and higher quality.

• Become more productive.

The push toward reengineering going on in corporations around the country, and indeed, around the world, is most fundamentally an effort to improve productivity. By removing unnecessary steps in the work and production processes, companies become more productive.

Improving productivity provides companies with greater flexibility to deal with competitive pressures.

7

Assessing the Competition

153

**• Develop
a competitor
matrix.**

The what-if questions are part of the process of planning your competitor responses. Another part is comparing yourself with competitors systematically. A chart, or matrix, that illustrates how all direct and key industry competitors compare is an excellent way to develop an aggressive approach to handling the competition. The most appropriate criteria are those that define your product and your place in your industry—such matters as price, product or service features, and company size.

One of the best matrices I've seen is the one done by CareerTrack (see Exhibit 7–1, page 159). It compares competitors on the basis of 11 criteria that it determined to be key service and industry measurements.

Frookies constructed a much simpler chart to compare itself to competitors on the basis of price (see Exhibit 7–2, page 168). It concluded "that Frookies will be positioned midway in price among its competitors, but with a unique appeal."

When you look at yourself in the midst of such a matrix, you can quickly determine where you stand out and where you blend in. Most important, you can question the appropriateness of the differences and similarities from a planning viewpoint.

Your Competitive Advantage

From knowledge comes power. The more you know about the competition, the more informed and confident will be your own moves on the competitive battlefield. It isn't so much what your competitors are doing, but what you are doing better than competitors. In other words, what are your competitive advantages? Why will prospective customers buy from you rather than from your competitors? How clearly, and on what basis, do prospects distinguish you from the competition?

You may decide to distinguish yourself on the basis of particular criteria, emphasizing, for example, the length of time you have been in business if most of your competitors are young, or your dependability if many competitors have gone out of business.

Or you may decide to add product or service features based on some successes direct competitors are having. If you discover that a competitor offering next-day delivery or a longer warranty is rapidly adding customers, and can obtain evidence that such a feature is largely responsible, you must ask yourself whether you need to do the same thing—and perhaps more.

Or you may decide that your competitors don't do a very good job and that you should ignore them and keep doing what you do best.

The best way to achieve competitive advantage is by offering the best overall value. That comes across in CareerTrack's assessment of its competitive advantages (see Exhibit 7–1, page 160). Among many that are described is a key one of "Top-Caliber Trainers." The plan observes, "CareerTrack offers a low-priced seminar that is generally of much higher quality than its competitors'. The main reason is that CareerTrack can afford to employ the best trainers in the industry (including many who used to be top trainers for CareerTrack's competitors)." The plan then lists a number of advantages and incentives it provides to attract and motivate trainers to give the company an edge.

Clearly, the company understands the driving forces and economics of its business that it can confidently compare itself to competitors. That is the best way to make use of competitive data.

▶ Exercises

1. Identify your three most important direct, or segment, competitors.

2. Name your three most significant industry competitors.

3. Identify and describe at least two indirect competitors.

4. Imagine that a major direct competitor has significantly cut its prices. Describe two possible responses from you, neither of which entails cutting prices.

5. List the four most important "what if" questions regarding competitors' actions.

6. Describe four ways in which you regularly obtain information about competitors.

7. Name the two most important pieces of competitive information you don't have but would like to have.

8. Specify two potential (legal) approaches to obtain that information.

9. Describe at least two things competitors are doing that you admire and would consider applying in your company.

10. Develop a competitor matrix for your company.

11. Identify your company's four most important competitive advantages.

(Worksheets for this chapter are provided on page 287)

EXHIBIT 7-1

FROM THE MARKETING PLAN OF
★ CAREERTRACK ★

COMPETITION

The seminar production segment of the human resources development industry is highly fragmented. According to the editors of *Training and Development Journal,* more than 6,000 companies in the U.S. engage in some aspect of seminar production. The majority of companies in the industry are small firms with a limited number of employees and limited annual revenues. Typically, but not always, these companies are consulting firms specializing in a particular industry or human resources problem. By contrast, CareerTrack is the largest company of its kind in the industry, with over 425 employees and over $66 million in annual revenue. In addition to corporate-sponsored seminars, there are approximately 100 to 150 colleges and universities that offer continuing education courses on professional development subjects.

CareerTrack's management has identified the following organizations as its most direct competition:

- Dun & Bradstreet's Education Services Division (D&B), New York, New York.
- National Seminars, Inc. (Division of Rockhurst College), Shawnee Mission, Kansas.
- Path Management Industries, Inc. (Division of AMA), Shawnee Mission, Kansas.
- Pryor Resources Corporation, Shawnee Mission, Kansas.

7

Assessing the Competition

In addition, there are several organizations that compete with CareerTrack as members of the training industry, although indirectly because of the products and services they offer (these competitors produce high-priced, multi-day seminars):

- American Management Association, Inc. (AMA),
  New York, New York.
- Dale Carnegie & Associates, Inc., Garden City, New York.

The matrix on the following page compares key information from the aforementioned firms and others.

COMPETITOR MATRIX
Updated 01/15/92

COMPANY	Founding Date	1991 Estimated Revenue ($ Millions)	1991 Estimated Number Of Programs	1991 Estimated Number Of Attendees	1991 Estimated Number Of Cities	Seminar Price Range (U.S. DOLLARS)	Seminar Price Average	Seminar Length	Seminar Size Range	Seminar Size Average	Est. # of Employees
AMA [4]	1972	150	6,600	165,000	100+	$775–$5,000	$895	3–5 days	15–40	25	975
Dale Carnegie	1912	150	6,100	215,000	250+	$595–$795	$695	8 sessions	30–40	35	300
CareerTrack	1982	65	4,200	600,000	600	$39–$195	$65	1 day [3]	100–300	135	415
Path Management [4]	1985 [1]	55	5,000	450,000	400	$69–$395	$99	1 day	75–100	90	175
National [4]	1984	38	4,500	400,000	400	$49–$149	$99	1 day	75–150	90	135
Pryor Resources	1975	26	3,000	260,000	400	$59–$195	$99	1 day	50–200	85	100
D&B [2][4]	1983	20	2,700	200,000	300	$99–$165	$125	1 day	25–100	75	100
Seminars Intl.	1986	8	1,500	65,000	100	$79–$115	$115	1 day	25–75	50	25
SkillPath	1989	7.5	1,500	125,000	200	$49–$199	$99	1 day	50–100	75	50
Performance Sem	1972	7	800	28,000	100	$225–$295	$250	1 day	25–50	35	30
Totals before smaller competitor and colleges/universities		526.5	35,900	2,508,000							

(1) Path Management is a holding company of four divisions, some of which were founded as early as 1979 and purchased by AMA in 1990.
(2) D&B is a division of Dun & Bradstreet.
(3) Approximately 5% of CareerTrack's seminars are 2-day, $195 programs.
(4) These seminar companies are now part of non-profit organizations.
(5) Many companies, other than CareerTrack, employ additional temporary workers during peak times of enrollment activity.

7

Assessing the Competition

EXHIBIT 7-1
continued

STRENGTHS/COMPETITIVE ADVANTAGES

CareerTrack has numerous competitive advantages
that are responsible for its continued growth, including:

Quality of Training

Seminar participants consistently rate CareerTrack's program content 8.3 on a scale of 1 to 10. CareerTrack's in-house program development staff is responsible for creating and maintaining the quality of CareerTrack's seminar offerings. CareerTrack's primary training programs were recently updated and standardized with concise curriculum guides for trainers to follow. A major indicator of the caliber of CareerTrack's programs is its annual refund rate of under 1%. (CareerTrack's trainers are discussed in detail below.)

Convenience and Affordability of Training

CareerTrack has an ongoing, worldwide schedule of public training programs. At any given time, the Company offers over 25 roll-out programs in 500 market areas in North America, and another 100 around the world. CareerTrack's breadth of topics and scheduling strategy makes it easy for customers to attend a variety of programs at convenient local sites. No other direct competitor of the Company's offers as many topics as frequently as does CareerTrack.

CareerTrack's registration fees have always been affordable. In 1982, CareerTrack introduced a $99, one-day seminar when the rest of the industry was charging $150 to $250 for similar programs. In 1985, when competitors matched the price, CareerTrack implemented a $45 fee. The average seminar price in 1991 was $60 (most seminars were priced at either the $49 or $99 price point). (The Company's exception to the low pricing structure are its

EXHIBIT 7–1
continued

two-day management seminars, which usually command a $195 or $295 fee.) Although other companies have tried to compete with CareerTrack on price, they cannot match the Company's profitability at low prices, because they have not developed CareerTrack's sophisticated ancillary profit centers (explained previously and again below).

CEU Certification

Many CareerTrack courses are accredited with individual state education boards and other niche industry associations as continuing education courses. These qualifications enable the Company to attract audience members looking to complete yearly requirements for continuing education.

Ancillary Profit Centers

For every public seminar registration, CareerTrack generates additional substantial revenue from back-of-the-room tape sales, private seminars and customer list rental. While CareerTrack's competitors have the same add-on revenue possibilities, they have not exploited their full potential.

Customer Verification

CareerTrack began an extensive "customer verification" program in 1990 to ensure the recency and quality of the names contained in its customer list. A team of 20 internally-employed customer verification representatives are responsible for verifying each and every record of CareerTrack's customer database. To date, over 350,000 of CareerTrack's 2 million active customers (last 36 months) have been verified.

Video Studio

CareerTrack's new $750,000 audio and video production studio enables the Company to eliminate costly production and post-production facility fees.

Assessing the Competition

EXHIBIT 7–1
continued

In-house production also allows for improved quality control and ease in making mid-production changes. Reshooting video segments is extremely costly when working out of house, but virtually free with in-house facilities.

Top-Caliber Trainers

CareerTrack offers a low-priced seminar that is generally of much higher quality than its competitors'. The main reason is that CareerTrack can afford to employ the best trainers in the industry (including many who used to be top trainers for CareerTrack's competitors). CareerTrack's faculty of over 100 trainers are under a comprehensive contract with CareerTrack (most of their business is with the Company). CareerTrack has attracted the best trainers as a result of the following:

- CareerTrack pays trainers a base rate of $400 to $750 per day, up to 100% more than its competitors.
- Trainers have the opportunity to add a range of $100 to $500 to their daily fee through sales commissions for products sold at seminars.
- CareerTrack offers its trainers the opportunity to publish audio and video tapes, which creates substantial royalties and personal visibility.
- Each trainer has the chance to develop and market his or her own seminars through the Company, which can generate up to $25,000 per year for the speaker.
- CareerTrack trainers have the opportunity to train internationally.
- CareerTrack has one of the most rigorous recruitment processes in the training industry. Only one trainer is hired for every 50 applicants. Once hired, trainers must maintain an average audience rating of 8.5 on a 10.0 scale (as stated, the current average is 9.0).

EXHIBIT 7-2

FROM THE MARKETING PLAN OF ★ *R.W. FROOKIES* ★

THE COMPETITION

There are dozens and dozens of cookies on the market. This summary is not intended as a fully comprehensive review of every major cookie producer. Instead, the producers below are included to provide a comparison with Frookies.

1. Nabisco (Approximately $1 billion in cookie sales; Oreos, a 16-ounce package retails for $2.19)[18]

With roughly 30% of the cookie market, Nabisco is the most well-known producer in the world and has the largest market share. Its "flagship cookie," the Oreo, has been on the market for 76 years. Nabisco, like other major producers such as Keebler and Duncan Hines, has tried to be a low-cost producer of high-volume, mass-marketed cookies. The company is now looking at worldwide marketing strategies—and still recovering from its 1985 merger with RJ Reynolds. There is no evidence to suggest that at this time, Nabisco or the other major producers are interested in or are philosophically or physically geared up to make a healthy, sugar-free cookie.

2. Archway ($40 million in annual sales, 12 ounces retail for $1.69)

Archway, as a medium sized "niche" company, provides an interesting role model for Frookies. This company has offered a "homestyle" soft cookie for 50 years. With the soft cookie wars of 1983, Nabisco, Proctor and Gamble, Keebler, and Frito Lay all entered the soft cookie market with massive ad campaigns. Archway was able to withstand the onslaught of the majors, and in fact, continued to grow—due to its good

---

[18]All prices listed in this section were obtained through a random survey of the Purity Supreme in Woburn, MA (a major chain store), and various health food stores during the period June 15–25, 1987.

reputation ("it tastes good") and intelligent advertising campaigns.

Likewise, if Frookies becomes successful, other major competitors will enter the market. Archway demonstrates that a company with a good quality "niche" product and an intelligent strategy can survive and benefit from increased advertising and competition.

3. Pepperidge Farm ($150 million in sales; 5$\frac{1}{2}$ ounce bag of cookies retails for $1.19)[19]

A division of Campbells Soup, Pepperidge Farm is well respected in the industry for providing a quality, attractively packaged product at an above average (but acceptable to the consumer) price point. In short, Pepperidge Farm shows that consumers will pay more for a good cookie. Pepperidge Farm cookie sales have been strong and the company has recently introduced several well-received new lines, such as the Chocolatier cookies and American Collection cookies. Based on discussions with people in the industry and reviews of annual reports and trade publications, Pepperidge Farm will continue to introduce good-quality, good-tasting foods in all of its product lines. What is not apparent is any current interest in the "natural, healthy foods" area.

Of all the current cookie producers, Frookies will be positioned similar to Pepperidge Farm. Like Pepperidge Farm, Frookies will offer several varieties of cookies around a common theme. The packaging for both companies (i.e. white backgrounds) is distinctive and attractive. Frookies will also be similar in terms of size and price point.

Frookies are unique, however, because of the emphasis on "sugar free and no cholesterol." Could Pepperidge Farm develop a new line of products to compete with Frookies? Certainly. Nevertheless, there is a substantial record that shows that the first food product into the market-

[19]Some of Pepperidge Farm's "specialty" cookies are 7$\frac{1}{2}$ oz, $1.89.

EXHIBIT 7-2
continued

place can retain its customer loyalty and expand its market in light of quality competition—as long as the product and approach to the market are good.

It also would be difficult for Pepperidge Farm, or other major producers, to properly position a sugar-free cookie in relation to their current product lines. Currently, Pepperidge Farm is doing a growing and profitable business exclusively with sugar-based cookies. If the company came out with a new, "healthy" sugar-free product, what would this say about its current line? Would Pepperidge Farm compete with itself and reduce the sales of its own cookies?

Smuckers, the market share leader in jams, faced the same dilemma when challenged by Sorrell Ridge's sugar-free product line. After several years of procrastination, Smucker's introduced a lower quality, "low sugar" jam which has not made a substantial impact in the market.

Frookies will *not* be the first fruit-juice sweetened, 'all natural" cookie on the market. Frookies can be easily differentiated from the following fruit-juice sweetened cookies:

Barbara's Cookies (Approximately $4 million in sales; 5 ounces, $1.55)

This company was started by two women who sold out to Wheatabix two years ago. As a division of Wheatabix, Barbara's markets a whole range of "health oriented" products including cereals, potato chips, and sweeteners.

There are substantial "concept" differences between Barbara's Cookies and Frookies. In short, Barbara's offers a "health food cookie," while Frookies is a good-tasting, high-quality cookie designed for the mass market—which also happens to be healthy and good for you. The differences are described below:

Assessing the Competition

165

EXHIBIT 7-2

continued

- Barbara's uses health food ingredients not widely accepted by the mass market (i.e. whole wheat flour). The cookie is more geared to vegetarian tastes and is somewhat bland compared to Frookies.
- Barbara's cookies are small (about $1^{1}/_{4}$ inch in diameter) and irregular shaped—not typical of the mass market. Frookies will be larger (2 inches in diameter) and look more like a "normal" cookie.
- Barbara's has a limited variety of cookies. Frookies will have 5–7 varieties, all duplicating accepted cookie types.
- Barbara's name and packaging are reminiscent of a "1960s" health food style. Frookies, though oriented towards health quality, is not a "neo-hippie" cookie.
- The 5-ounce size bag of Barbara's cookies is simply too small to justify munching. Frookies will offer more food at comparable cost.
- Barbara's is marketed almost exclusively in health food stores— and in some health food sections of the supermarkets. Frookies will be in the cookie section of supermarkets.

In spite of these drawbacks, Barbara's Cookies has succeeded in obtaining significant shelf space in natural food stores and increasing its sales. Barbara's demonstrates that the consumer is ready for a fruit-juice sweetened cookie.

It is difficult to predict how much additional development and marketing will be devoted to Barbara's Cookies. It should be noted, however, that Wheatabix is primarily a cereal manufacturer and is undoubtedly most interested in promoting Barbara's line of cereals. With the widely diversified Barbara's product line, it is doubtful that Wheatabix would place substantial energy in one segment—the cookie area. Frookies will not spread itself too thin and will fully exploit its one product, cookies.

EXHIBIT 7-2
continued

Pride of the Farm (Approximately 2\frac{1}{2}$ million in sales, 9 ounce bag for $1.59)

This new company entered the market with a fruit-juice sweetened cookie 1$\frac{1}{2}$ years ago. The product is fairly good, but the packaging is primitive and clearly targeted to the "health conscious." Pride of the Farm is sold exclusively in natural food stores. The quick success of this product is a further indication of the pent-up demand for a healthy "good for you" cookie.

Nature's Warehouse (Approximately 2\frac{1}{2}$ million in sales, 9 ounce bag for $1.59)

The product and packaging for Nature's Warehouse is very similar to Pride of the Farm. Nature's Warehouse has a variety of natural food products and has recently moved sideways, into sugar-free candy. Because this company has diversified, Nature's Warehouse has weakened its ability to saturate the cookie market and extend beyond health food stores.

Famous Amos ($50 million in annual sales; 5 ounces, $3.50)

The "gourmet" cookie food category is perhaps best exemplified by Famous Amos. Other comparable premium cookies include David's cookies and Jenny's Cookies. This category has grown rapidly during the last several years and shows the public's desire for a premium, high-quality product. The willingness to pay a price more than *triple* that of conventional cookies shows that consumers will pay for a unique product. Frookies will be positioned much lower in price than "gourmet" cookies—an elegant, upscale cookie that is still everyday affordable.

7

Assessing the
Competition

EXHIBIT 7-2
continued

A FINAL COMMENT: PRICE AND THE COMPETITION

Below is a summary of the cookies described in this section. Also included is a survey of the pricing structure of the jam market.

Cookies

Product	Market Orientation		Retail Price
Oreos	dependable brand name	16 oz.	$2.19
Archway	dependable brand name	12 oz.	$1.69
Pepperidge Farm	good quality cookie	5.5 oz.	$1.19
Famous Amos	gourmet cookie	5 oz.	$3.50
FROOKIES	good quality, upscale perception, healthy, no sugar	7 oz.	$1.69
Barbara's Cookies*	no sugar, health food orientation	5 oz.	$1.55
Pride of the Farm	no sugar, health food orientation	9 oz.	$1.59
Nature's Warehouse	no sugar, health food orientation	9 oz.	$1.59

Strawberry Jams**

Product	Market Orientation		Retail Price
Smucker's	dependable brand name	12 oz.	$1.39
Kraft	dependable brand name	18 oz.	$1.79
Purity Supreme	generic store brand	12 oz.	$.99
Sorrell Ridge	good quality, no sugar	10 oz.	$1.59
Polaners	good quality, no sugar	10 oz.	$1.59
Smucker's Low Sugar	Smucker's response; contains some sugar, not as high in quality	10.15 oz.	$1.49
Trappist		12 oz.	$2.39

* Not placed in the cookie section of supermarkets.
** Prices are from shelf survey at Purity Supreme, Woburn, MA on June 29, 1987.

This summary shows that Frookies will be positioned midway in price among its competitors, but with a unique appeal. Sorrell Ridge has been successful with very similar market/price positioning.

PART III:

TAKING ACTION

COMMUNICATING WITH YOUR MARKET

The Growing Power of Information

I n this chapter I address how to make your plan happen, or implementation. The best plan in the world won't do you any good if you can't put it into effect; it must outline your plan of action.

You must first get the right messages out to your marketplace. This section of the marketing plan, on using information and technology, is where you put all those great ideas about target markets, positioning, and competitive strategy to the ultimate test—using them in the real world.

An example helps illustrate adept marketplace communication:

Each month, The Body Shop sends a half-hour video to the owners and managers of its more than 600 stores around the world to keep them and their employees up-to-date about the company. (Videos go out twice a month in the United States and weekly in the United Kingdom.)

A recent video begins by looking at the big picture. There are sales figures—company-wide and for new stores that have opened in the United States and Italy. Future plans are revealed for downsized stores to service smaller towns in England. And there is founder Anita Roddick, inspiring and extolling the troops at a motivational meeting of store managers from around the world.

"How do we keep competitive in the tough retail environment?" she asks. She answers, "Information is power, information is knowledge."

The video then implicitly reinforces Roddick's point—with endless detailed information from headquarters in England as well as from store employees about serving customers better. In quick, professionally arranged sound bites, there is advice on using (and recycling) a new Father's Day display, on how to welcome customers ("with a bright friendly smile," suggests one employee), and on how to put together an effective window display ("get that light. . . right," advises a window designer).

At one point, when a headquarters' representative insists, for perhaps the fifth time in the video, that store windows be kept clean, a female voice interjects: "If you say, 'Clean your window and base' one more time, we will run out into the street and scream." Another female voice responds: "When the day dawns that every window in every Body Shop shines clean like a good deed in a naughty world, then and only then will [the headquarters' rep] stop saying, 'Clean your base and window thoroughly.' "

At The Body Shop, for all its respect and fame, it comes down, symbolically, to clean windows. And well it should. Anita Roddick understands that clean windows (along with polished floors, shiny brass, attractive product displays, pleasant smells, and other small details) are part of a total package that attracts customers and gives the company an advantage over competitors. "It's serious stuff out there," she says of a retail environment in which many famous names have fallen by the wayside.

Roddick is keenly aware that no detail is too small to be worthy of attention. She also understands that no detail affecting interactions with customers is too small to be properly communicated to those out in the field—over and over again.

Indeed, The Body Shop is a master of using information for marketing advantage. By making detailed, entertaining information available to individuals running Body Shop stores, the company enables them to improve the service they offer customers and increase sales. The effort doesn't end with the videos, though. The company reenforces its message in as many ways as possible—through a newsletter for employees, in pamphlets, on carryout bags, and via displays directed at shoppers.

The Body Shop's skill in using information symbolizes the growing importance of communicating innovatively and effectively with prospects and customers. All companies that want to succeed need to communicate in ever more sophisticated ways with their markets and the people who serve them.

But how do you know which information and approaches work best to implement the strategy you have chosen? This chapter helps you select from among a variety of techniques to maximize your company's communications.

Which Information Is Key?

There is no shortage of techniques for communicating with the marketplace. These include advertising, public relations, direct mail, events sponsorship, and newsletters, among many others; a number are discussed later in this chapter. But before you can intelligently decide how best to communicate with your market, first determine which information is essential to achieving your company's marketing goals.

Among the key types of information to communicate are the following:

• Benefits information.

This is the most fundamental type of information from a marketing perspective, because marketing success hinges on the marketplace's perception of your product's or service's benefits. R.W. Frookies in its packaging and publicity touts its product as "the good for you cookie." Of course, cookies have traditionally been seen as a bad-for-you food. So, without saying anything about the product's ingredients, appearance, or other factors, the company conveys an important benefit.

In its promotional literature, R.W. Frookies similarly concentrates on benefits. The company's cookies are described in a press release as low in total sugar content because of its use of fruit and fruit juice (with most of the sugar content in the form of fructose). "Metabolic effects of pure fructose shows an even, slow rise in blood sugar. On the other hand, table sugar (sucrose) rapidly boosts blood sugar and requires the body to produce large amounts of insulin to return blood sugar to a normal level."

The financial gains possible from using MicroFridge microwaves-refrigerators-freezers in hotels, discussed at length in Chapter 5 (and excerpted in Exhibit 5-2), are a particularly effective use of benefits information. The company distributes a "Hotel/Motel Purchase Justification" that takes prospective customers through a calculation of the potential gains.

This is descriptions of product or service attributes—which most of us think of first when asked to describe our products or services. This information is being used to increasing advantage by companies seeking to stand out in their industries.

• Product/ service infor- mation.

Some companies use such information to distinguish themselves from lower-quality competitors. Smartfoods on its packaging combines product information and humor in explaining how its cheddar cheese popcorn is made and how it is superior to the competition:

> "Unlike some naughty companies who do mean and nasty things to their popcorn, we treat our kernels with the love and respect that real food deserves. We DON'T drown our kernels in oil and preservatives. That wouldn't be fair. . . they can't swim.
>
> "We DON'T make our kernels wear funny looking colors. Let's face it, it's embarrassing! Besides, bright orange cheese isn't normal.
>
> "As for artificial flavor, we DON'T let our kernels roll around in that stuff. It spoils the natural taste of delicious popcorn.
>
> "What we DO is combine fresh, air-popped popcorn with the best corn oil and the most delicious WHITE cheddar cheese seasoning to create a totally wholesome and delight-ful product."

Some companies use product-related information to build confidence and suggest additional uses for the prod-

175

uct. The Body Shop does both in distributing more than a dozen informational brochures to shoppers in its stores. There are brochures on skin, hair, the sun, and smell, among many others. These provide information about the subject being discussed and how The Body Shop products fit into the overall scheme of things.

The brochure about smell explains its role in our current lives and in history. ("Written records of the use of fragrances stretch back over 3,000 years. The Assyrian Book of Herbs, written around 2,000 BC, contains recipes for medicinal herb mixtures and for fragrant oils and perfumes, including a scented drink to combat bad breath.") It also discusses how smells can bring back good and bad memories and how the human nose can detect more than 10,000 different smells.

All the observations about smell make the brochure's more provocative statements about the competition seem just additional pieces of information. "A designer label often guarantees a new perfume arrives with a ready-made public profile," observes a section on "Designer Smells" (see Exhibit 8–1, page 202). "There are many people who want to buy a scent with a designer's name on it, even though it is accompanied by layers of expensive, wasteful packaging, and is marketed and hyped to the limit. . . . But many others prefer to follow The Body Shop route." There follows information about the absence of animal extracts, the use of minimal packaging, and the value in The Body Shop's perfume products.

That isn't all, however. The brochure follows up with suggestions on where to dab perfume on your body, how to use it in your home, and how to perfume notepaper. It represents adroit use of information, cleverly designed to encourage you to buy and use as much of the company's products as possible.

The people who are out in the field doing your selling, whether manufacturers' reps, your own sales force, retailers, or distributors, need as much information as possible about what works and what doesn't in the selling process. This information may be as basic as product literature and a few sales leads.

• Sales information.

The goal, though, should be to provide sophisticated and useful information and tools to your sales outlets. These may include instructions to retailers on displaying a product for maximum effectiveness, possibly even including the actual display racks, such as those provided by book publishers to bookstores or by toothpaste distributors to discount drugstore chains (point-of-purchase displays).

The Body Shop's videos are among the more sophisticated approaches for communicating sales information. We can expect that sophistication to continue, possibly including multimedia displays that salespeople can view on their computers.

This is the data you maintain about your prospects and customers, which may be saved on databases. Wall Street Games does an excellent job of maintaining infor-

• Prospect/ customer information.

8

Communicating
with Your Market

mation about its customers, relying on a list of more than 100,000 people who have had contact with the company—as contestants or as inquirers about participating in an Investment Challenge (a three-month contest of stock picking by entrants).

How Do You Use the Information?

There is no one right or wrong answer. Ideally, though, you use the information you have about your company and its performance to learn from your mistakes and improve your communication.

At Wall Street Games, company executives putting together a marketing information plan examine the database to learn what percentage of past customers came in from advertisements, college campus selling efforts, articles developed from public relations, and direct-mail campaigns—and plan upcoming events accordingly. They also sample opinions on college campuses about factors that don't come through on database results, such as reactions to ads or the effectiveness of the company's on-campus representatives.

As the executives focus on particular approaches—advertising or college promotions, for example—they determine which ads or college reps were most or least successful in the past, and consequently adjust their communications effort. Sometimes, in asking questions, they find they don't have the information they need to provide a satisfactory answer, so they adjust their information gathering accordingly.

The adjustments made for the Fourth Annual AT&T Collegiate Investment Challenge are spelled out in Wall Street Games' marketing plan for the event in 1991 (see Exhibit 8–2, page 205). "After polling students and professors, prior creative efforts have been perceived as AT&T image advertising and not an effective Collegiate Investment Challenge message. In response to the creative message needed to sell this product WSG has teamed with American Passage (a collegiate direct selling specialist), and our own in-house ad agency to bring the message to a new creative level." A new ad, with the heading, "BE A PLAYER! . . . in the ultimate Wall Street game," is shown at the end of the plan. This ad attempts to capture the drama of readers successfully buying and selling stocks, and downplays the involvement of AT&T and other corporate sponsors.

The plan also notes that its information gathering pointed up "a significant lack of awareness on campus of the Challenge." Additional promotion is needed, the plan concludes: "This program includes registration deadlines, consistent creative messages, limited participation (currently limited to 20,000 participants), free premium offers (a Wall Street poster) and intense material distribution."

Two other steps planned to improve awareness are an upgrading of the company's on-campus representation and a targeted effort to collect information concerning campus promotional efforts. The company will "enlist the best on-campus sponsors available (unlike prior years when any person on a campus was good enough)." In addition, "Proposed is a system that will cumulatively track contacts and sales information and allow us to renew the successful [on-campus] sponsors (and drop unsuccessful sponsors) for future years."

The information the company stores on its computers also helps it plan its hiring. Executives know from past Investment Challenge contests the pace of entries and trading. They can use that information to plan how many students to hire for various shifts to man the dozens of computer terminals at which information is collected and monitored. Students are trained to ask callers certain questions about where they heard or read about the Investment Challenge, so

8

Communicating
with Your Market

the information is constantly updated. Moreover, the computer system must replicate the functions of a full-service brokerage firm, enabling entrants to monitor stock quotations and buy and sell stocks with ease.

Sometimes you hit on ways to use information effectively and simply keep doing more of it. As noted earlier, both Syms and The Body Shop are believers in communicating product and industry information as a way to spark the interest and build the confidence of customers. Yet Syms depends nearly exclusively on radio and television commercials to convey how it can afford to discount its merchandise. Its experiments with magazine and newspaper ads haven't been particularly effective, so the company sticks with what works.

The Body Shop has avoided advertising of all types (in favor of public relations). That stems from Anita Roddick's aversion to the cosmetics industry's traditional means of promoting its products. But at the same time, avoiding advertising also fits in with the company's image of being a rebel in its industry. In a perverse way, by avoiding advertising the company helps maintain its position as a supremely honest company that, according to Roddick, "sells health instead of glamour."

A few guideposts about the role of information in implementing your marketing plan:

• Information really is power. Information comes in many forms and, for executives, one challenge is recognizing which information is most important for communicating effectively with the marketplace—and capturing it for future use. Key information may include lists of prospective customers who have inquired about your product to endorsements from satisfied customers.

Such information should be collected in an orderly and systematic way, because it can often be used as a selling tool. For example, people who have inquired about your product or service, even if they haven't made purchases, often represent legitimate sales leads that should be followed up. They may be worth contacting in a subsequent direct-mail or telemarketing campaign. Similarly, letters praising a product can sometimes be used to great effect in sales literature or advertising.

In every industry, conventional wisdom dictates how one should go about selling various products and services. Traditionally, soap, cars, cereals, and assorted other mass merchandise have been promoted through TV and radio commercials and in print media ads. Likewise, newsletters and magazines have been sold through direct mail, while clothes, flowers, and wine have been marketed through retail outlets.

• Beware of the conventional wisdom.

The fact of the matter is, traditional forms of conveying information have become less effective. That helps explain why major corporations are searching out alternatives to TV commercials and increasingly resorting to other approaches like direct mail. And why sellers of items traditionally sold through direct mail, like magazines, are using spots on cable television. And why retail items are being distributed via direct mail.

To stand out from competitors, companies need to try new approaches to selling.

8

Communicating
with Your Market

• Opportunities for creativity abound.

Many of the most successful executives of the 1990s are thriving based not only on ignoring the conventional wisdom but on devising creative alternatives to it. In that context, The Body Shop has succeeded because it has developed some less obvious ways of communicating with its marketplace. For instance, the company has used public relations—ranging from articles in the business press to television interviews with Anita Roddick to open houses for the press at British headquarters—to obtain publicity with much more credibility than any advertising campaign could provide. With the money it saves by not advertising, it is free to concentrate more intensively on public relations. And by being so active in environmental and other causes, the company has ensured that it has a story interesting enough that the press will give it attention.

• New communications options are available.

Rapidly advancing technology allows growing companies to communicate with customers and prospects in new ways. Options range from local cable-television stations to CD-ROM to the so-called Information Superhighway.

We don't yet have enough experience with them to make definitive statements about their bottom-line advantages. However, I get excited by nearly any new approaches for communicating with markets.

For businesses that focus on local markets, cable television can be an excellent communications option. Most communities have a cable-television station, and many stations have interview and other programs that need to be filled with guests, company examples, and information about local events.

Retailers and mail-order sellers of computer software are using CD-ROMs to offer prospective customers previews of software. Customers who want to purchase a particular program call the seller, provide their credit-card numbers, and are given a code to unlock the actual program on the CD-ROM.

The most exciting communications options may be emerging on the Information Superhighway. On computer services like Internet, CompuServe, and Prodigy, users are able to preview business and consumer magazines, order financial reporting services, and even order full-length books via modem. Additional services and communications approaches are becoming available as the popularity of these services grows.

The Key Communication Options: Advantages and Disadvantages

Clearly, there is no shortage of communication options available to executives. Indeed, the larger challenge is selecting among the various alternatives.

One thing is certain, though: No magic potion exists. Each communication vehicle has its advantages and disadvantages. Here is a quick review of the main approaches:

Many executives, when they think of communicating information to potential buyers, think first of advertising.

• **Advertising.**

That is only natural because it is the vehicle we are all exposed to most frequently.

Advantages: The main attraction of advertising is that the message can be controlled. You can place an ad in anything from a mass-circulation newspaper to an exclusive industry trade journal and convey whatever message you want. You can use words, pictures, drawings, or graphs. You can be cute or serious.

In addition, you can select publications most likely to reach your target market, since most media outlets keep close tabs on such matters as the ages, incomes, and purchasing habits of their readers. With the array of special-interest and industry publications, it is possible to reach any of hundreds of target markets.

Disadvantages. Advertising during the recession of the early 1990s fell into some disfavor because of two principal problems. For one thing, it is generally very expensive—up to $80,000 or more for a full-page ad in a national newspaper or magazine and even more for television commercials on prime-time programs. For another, it is often difficult to measure the effectiveness of advertising. Sure, for certain products or services it is possible to include coupons or provide telephone numbers for inquiries to measure responses. But in the majority of situations when that isn't practical, such as when manufacturers are running ads for products purchased through retailers, the actual impact of advertising is often not known.

PR involves media exposure in any of a number of forms—news articles about your company, quotes of its officials, bylined articles by company executives in trade journals, and interviews on radio and television. It differs from advertising in that you don't pay the publication for the exposure (though in some industry publications or among smaller media outlets, news exposure is provided more readily to advertisers than to nonadvertisers).

Advantages. The advantage of PR over advertising is that the media exposure you receive has greater credibility than a paid advertisement. Readers tend to find references to companies in articles or interviews more believable than those in ads.

Public relations is also usually less expensive than advertising. While there is often a tendency to consider news media exposure "free," there is a cost associated with getting articles and interviews. The cost may come in the form of executive or other employee time given over to public relations or from fees paid to a PR firm.

Disadvantages. With advertising, companies have complete control over the media's message, but with public relations, companies lose control of the message. Control is in the hands of reporters and editors, who are less interested in positioning your company the way you want and more interested in appealing to reader or viewer interests and emotions. In worst cases, the message that's delivered about your company, which you portrayed so positively, comes out negative. For instance, if you announce plans for

• **Public relations.**

8

Communicating with Your Market

185

a new plant, an enterprising reporter might ferret out opposition from residents living in the area or from competitors, and cast an article as a battle over zoning or environmental issues.

The benefits of public relations are also difficult to measure. Unless individuals call up after seeing an article or hearing an interview and become customers or prospects, it can easily be assumed that the PR effort provided no benefit. However, people often clip articles and use them later, when they're in a position to buy. And when that time comes, they typically do not refer to the article of a few weeks or months ago and, unless the prospects are prodded as to what drove the purchase decision, the company may never learn about the benefits of public relations. Effective PR can also help in building name recognition for a product or service, giving greater impact to advertising or direct-mail promotions.

• Direct mail.

This is commonly referred to as junk mail. It typically consists of a catalog, a brochure, or a letter (as part of a "package" that includes a flyer, response card, and other supporting material). As noted earlier in this chapter, assorted sellers of products and services ranging from automobiles to insurance to flowers have begun using direct mail during the 1980s and 1990s.

Advantages. The most important advantage is that the results can be clearly quantified. If you mail out 50,000 pieces of direct mail at a cost of $25,000 and get 1,000 orders of a $50 product, or $50,000 of revenue, you know immediately that particular effort netted you $25,000. What could be more clear-cut? In addition, you will have learned that effort had a 2% response rate (1,000 responses from 50,000 inquiries), which makes planning for future direct-mail efforts easier.

Another advantage is that you can target your efforts precisely, since there are lists available for any of thousands of categories. You can rent or otherwise obtain lists of members of particular organizations, residents of a specific geographic area, or individuals holding certain management positions. Then you can determine which lists work best and fine-tune your future efforts.

Finally, it is possible to test a number of approaches and lists on a very small, low-cost basis. Moreover, such tests can be done discreetly, so that you lower the odds of competitors learning about your ideas.

Disadvantages. Not long ago users of direct-mail promotions could reasonably expect some minimum percentage returns from their efforts—say, 1% or 2%. They could then predict whether the direct-mail effort was worth their while. All that has changed. No longer are there any guarantees about direct-mail response rates.

Also, the costs have gone way up because of postal rate increases. During the 1980s it was possible to get per-letter costs (including design, printing, and postage) down to 30 cents or 35 cents each, while in the 1990s it became hard to do them for much less than 50 cents apiece.

And while direct mail looks easy to do, the catalogs,

8

Communicating with Your Market

letters, and other supporting material must be expertly crafted for best results. Two different direct-mail packages may have widely varying response rates, depending on their overall messages and appearances. It is usually advisable to hire a professional copywriter and designer to put a package together.

• **Marketing communications.** This is a catchall for a number of do-it-yourself communication-related techniques to impress customers, prospects, suppliers, and others. These techniques include newsletters, brochures, information booklets, and videos, along with sponsorship of events (seminars, golf tournaments, etc.) and award programs (for the best suppliers or industry achievers).

Marketing communications has become increasingly popular during the 1990s, as desktop publishing and compact video cameras have made producing newsletters and other publications easier and less costly. Organizations ranging from supermarkets to wine stores to accounting firms to hospitals now produce informational newsletters for customers, suppliers, and prospects.

Advantages. Like advertising, the message put out via marketing communications can be totally controlled by the company. Indeed, it's usually possible to include a much longer message in a newsletter or booklet than in an ad. Ideally, the message is information oriented rather than pure promotion, so your business is identified with conveying useful information. The implicit message is that you know your business so well that potential buyers should deal with you to ensure they get what they need. For businesses that are uncomfortable advertising—like law and accounting firms—marketing communications is highly desirable.

Thanks to the technological advances noted, marketing communications is also usually less expensive than advertising. And, like direct mail, it can be targeted to exactly the audience you want to reach.

Disadvantages. The very ease of doing marketing communications often leads to the biggest problem: poorly written and produced materials. Desktop publishing can make anyone feel like a graphic designer, but most of us aren't very accomplished. Also, it is easy to focus on the product of marketing communication—the newsletter, brochure, or video—without thinking much about how it will be distributed. There is nothing worse than taking delivery of 10,000 newsletters and then wondering who to send them to. Clearly, lists must be drawn up before putting together a newsletter.

Presumably, you have one or more distribution channels for your product or service—an in-house sales force, sales representatives, or mass distribution like retail outlets. If you are still pondering this matter, here are some brief guidelines: An in-house sales force is most appropriate for products/services that sell in quantities worth $10,000 or more; sales reps are best for products/services

• Distribution channels support.

Communicating with Your Market

8

that cost $1,000 to $10,000; and mass distribution is best for products/services under $1,000.

Distribution channels support can come in any of several forms. You may provide training and printed product literature to your sales force or reps, point-of-purchase displays to retailers, or instructional videos to your retailers (as The Body Shop has done).

Advantages. Your goal is to provide the information, education, and motivation to enable those who sell to do their jobs more effectively. Not only does successful support translate into higher sales, it also translates into improved morale of sellers, which can raise sales even further.

Disadvantages. Distribution channels support is often quite expensive. For example, sales training can cost hundreds of dollars a day for each salesperson trained. Mistakes are costly. A point-of-purchase display that doesn't work for retailers can be quickly relegated to the scrap heap, at a cost of many thousands of dollars. A common mistake is to institute an inappropriate sales incentive plan. If salespeople earn too little, they become discouraged. If they earn too much, from the owners' viewpoint, the plan may be scaled back and demoralize the salespeople.

Distribution channels support, then, should be carefully thought out. If possible, it should be tested on a small scale before launching it throughout your distribution channels.

Guerrilla Marketing:
Getting the Biggest Bang for Your Buck

Anyone who begins exploring information options will quickly discover ad agencies, PR firms, copywriting concerns, direct-mail companies, sales training firms, and other businesses eager to provide services at substantial fees. The shock that many executives experience when they explore the conventional approaches has led an increasing number to try unconventional approaches, with sometimes spectacular results.

Out of such experiences has evolved the term guerrilla marketing, which came into vogue during the late 1980s. One of its earliest adherents was Ken Meyers, a founder of Smartfoods. He describes the experience that led him to look for new kinds of solutions to common marketing challenges:

"We kind of fell into the guerrilla marketing thing. This was largely because we had very little money. We learned the hard way early on that the dollars wouldn't go nearly as far as I had imagined they would."

As noted in Chapter 1, advertising agencies recommended that the company commit to a four-week radio-advertising campaign costing about $87,000, which would have left the company with no resources for the other forty-eight weeks. "So we decided at that point that conventional means, as we knew them, didn't appear to be the way to go."

Meyers recalls, "We sort of regrouped, looked at our resources, and remembered that our greatest marketing tool was our package. In fact, it was already working to some degree in the supermarkets."

So the company built a campaign around its distinctive black-and-yellow packaging. Individuals dressed as Smartfood packages were hired to ski down New England ski slopes. Vans painted in the Smartfood colors went to parades, races, beaches, and anywhere crowds gathered to entertain con-

8

Communicating
with Your Market

sumers with comical skits and distribute small sample bags of the popcorn. "We would run onto the beaches with trash bags full of product, hand them out, and get chased off the beaches by the lifeguards," says Meyers.

The first guerrilla marketing event Meyers conceived occurred over Labor Day weekend of 1985: "I called in all my chits. I contacted friends from the Maine coast all the way down to the Connecticut shore and arranged for them to appear at predetermined times with trash bags full of sample product at every major beach along the entire New England coastline. Then I hired a plane to pull a Smartfood banner along the entire New England coastline, timed so that when my friends saw the plane fly overhead, they would hand out the product. We had 52 trash bags of 200 samples each, roughly 10,000 samples passed out along the entire coastline within three hours."

As sales grew, Meyers hired someone to focus on finding where Smartfoods could show up and hand out samples. "The objective was to get product into the hands of as many consumers as possible in a manner that would be memorable."

Over the next few years, "This guerrilla marketing thing began to heat up. It became our principal marketing vehicle. We would show up at other people's events and sometimes get involved as second- or third-level sponsors, but rarely for a fee. I think that in our seven years, we spent less than $7,000 in sponsorship fees for all of the events that we ever attended. We would say to event organizers, 'Hey, look, the road race you have going already has a major sponsor and we are a small company that doesn't have any marketing money, but we do have popcorn and we would love to give you and your patrons free samples.' Popcorn goes with most everything, so most of the time they welcomed us.

"We would arrive with one of our teams in a van filled with product. Some of these vans, called Comedy Cruisers, had rooftop stages where costumed dancers or standup comics would entertain while teams passed out samples to gathering crowds. Often, major sponsors would be frustrated by the end of an event because Smartfoods, generating most of the excitement, attracted most of the attention. The trick here is to capture your consumers' hearts and minds, at the same time you are capturing their tastebuds. If you can get them in a positive frame of mind while they are receiving your product and if you can capture their attention, you have created a memorable experience. The more memorable the experience, the more valuable it becomes."

Meyers feels that, on a cost-per-person basis, the exposure he arranged was more expensive than conventional advertising. But he is convinced that such exposure was much more effective. "By making introduction to Smartfood a memorable experience, we created a group of new-product missionaries—people who went out and started lots of little word-of-mouth brushfires. That was our most effective marketing tool."

There was another advantage in the Smartfoods approach, says Meyers: "If we had relied on ads and coupons, as many of the industry players did, we would have been judged to be largely the same as them. Our personality was developed through our marketing activities at the street level—underground marketing that gave us a cultish following. People feel a much stronger kinship to a product if they've had direct, positive interaction with the company."

Clearly, guerrilla marketing can provide important advantages:

• **Cost-effectiveness.**

As Smartfoods' experience suggests, guerrilla marketing approaches aren't necessarily cheap, but they allow for a bigger bang for your buck. Measured in terms of quantity—cost per person reached—the expenditures were high, but measured in quality—the intensity and importance of the contact—the guerrilla approach was more effective.

193

In some cases, guerrilla marketing approaches really are cheaper, as when Jackson Hewitt Tax Service, a Virginia Beach, Va., company with more than $14 million in annual revenues, decided to jettison its ad agency and bring the work in-house. John Hewitt decided that because ad agencies make their money by receiving a percentage of billings, they have little incentive to get the best deal for their clients. He was able to bargain television and radio stations down significantly in the rates they charged during the normally slow first quarter—which is his company's most important quarter.

With both agencies he employed, Hewitt feels it took two years to bring them up to speed on the nuances of the tax service business. "With an agency, there's always a learning curve. They have to understand who we're after. Agencies tend to talk in terms of age groups and income levels." Yet the fact is that 50% of the population, mostly blue-collar workers, files its returns between January 1 and February 20. "If you're not ready and you don't know who these people are, then you've lost 50% of your market right there," says Hewitt.

Hewitt says annual revenues have increased 10% and ad costs declined 10% since he began doing his own advertising. These savings compound each year.

• Competitive advantages. Guerrilla marketing tactics can also enable you to stand apart from the competition. As Meyers points out, the fact that Smartfoods wasn't distributing coupons and running ads like all the other snack food companies, but was being original and engaging with prospective customers, enabled the company to stand out from competitors.

Because guerrilla marketing techniques are inherently do-it-yourself, they tend to place marketers in more direct contact with prospects and customers. That closeness can pay double dividends: You sell more products and obtain feedback from the market, which enables you to devise techniques for broadening your appeal still further.

Take the case of Suntex, an Easton, Pa., game manufacturer. When it decided to roll out a new math game called Twenty-Four, in 1989, founder Robert Sun knew there was no way he could come up with the six-figure advertising budget that would make the large national chains give him shelf space.

Instead, Sun used a series of low-cost tournaments to build a base of players, increase distribution, and garner hundreds of thousands of dollars of free publicity. He got teachers, other educators, and businesspeople involved as well. In Chicago, a large local bank sponsored a citywide tournament in 1990 involving Twenty-Four. The tournament—in which hundreds of inner-city kids competed in a high-stakes game of mental arithmetic—was covered by four newspapers, five television stations, and six radio stations.

The results were immediate: Toys 'R' Us sold out of the product. Dominick's, a Chicago supermarket chain, sold 7,500 games that Christmas season. Its competitor,

• Closeness to the marketplace.

8

Communicating with Your Market

Eagle Foods, sold 3,000, and a major book chain in the area moved another 3,000. And Waldenbooks, one of the country's largest booksellers, crowned Twenty-Four its number-one-selling game that year.

After that, manufacturers, banks, and media outlets lined up to sponsor Twenty-Four Challenges in other cities. By the end of 1991 more than 400,000 copies of the game had been sold in two years, with revenues exceeding $1 million in 1991 alone. All that was accomplished at a fraction of the 15% of sales a traditional game marketer expects to spend on advertising.

Micromarketing: Moving Beyond the Conventional Wisdom

Guerrilla marketing is a great way for many companies to communicate with potential buyers cost-effectively. But all the books and articles written about it in recent years have in a sense served to make it part of the conventional wisdom.

These days, market-oriented companies are seeking unusual ways to communicate with their markets in an ongoing and more personal way. I refer to this trend as *micromarketing*. One of the outgrowths of this approach is for companies to establish organizations that include loyal customers as members. In the computer industry, user groups associated with Macintosh, Microsoft, and other hardware and software makers have been popular for some years. More recently, these companies have sought to plug into and formalize these groups. And outside the computer industry, the notion has taken hold. Harley-Davidson, the motorcycle maker, pushes the Harley Owners Group, which has more than 200,000 members worldwide. *The Utne Reader,* a magazine that reprints articles from unconventional publications, helps form subscriber discussion groups.

So-called cause-oriented marketing is another way to personalize the marketing communication process. The Body Shop's campaign against animal testing is a way to involve customers personally in a political cause while, not incidentally, garnering ongoing loyalty.

Professional service firms such as consulting and accounting firms have sought to engage in ongoing communications with their clients and prospects using newsletters and other written updates. The idea behind such communication devices is to continue the ongoing relationship, so that when recipients need a particular service they will think first of the firm sending the materials.

I see micromarketing moving to new levels, however, as companies discover new ways to go after customers, often nearly one at a time, build a relationship, and then use the relationship to spawn new relationships. Thus, a long-distance telephone company's campaign inviting customers to get discounts when they call friends and relatives who have the same telephone service is really an effort to get loyal customers to act as salespeople. It is hoped that the customers will persuade friends and relatives to switch phone services as a way to build market share.

Other companies that rely on word of mouth to attract customers seek to prime the pump by encouraging customers to spread the word. Sometimes they offer discounts to customers who bring new customers on board.

As companies accumulate data about the buying habits of their customers, expect to see new variations. Retailers that use bar codes and can identify customers know a great deal about individuals' buying habits. Thus, grocery chains are now in the position of being able to direct special offers for particular kinds of foods—say gourmet or low-fat items—to customers known to have bought significant quantities of such products.

The move to micromarketing is a reflection of the growing move toward customization and away from mass marketing. We can expect to see more variations on this theme as companies seek to understand and fulfill the needs of each customer.

The Best Approach for You

If there is one theme in this chapter, it is that there are a number of ways to communicate with your market, and it is up to you to find the right approach or combination of approaches. Here are some lessons that can be drawn from the experiences of companies discussed thus far:

1. Don't be afraid to experiment. The most successful techniques don't necessarily happen on the first try or from a single inspiration. If at all possible, experiment with approaches, make changes, and experiment some more. Despite what advertising or PR people tell you, there is no need to commit to substantial programs and budgets before you are sure of what works and doesn't work.

2. Determine what you need to control and what can be parceled out. Decisions about what to do in-house and when to hire outsiders should be based on a combination of cost-effectiveness and workability. There's nothing wrong with a patchquilt approach of having advertising and public relations done in-house and database management and direct mail handled by outsiders, or vice versa. The idea is to come up with the approach that works best for your particular situation.

It's rare that one or even two communication approaches will do the whole job for a product or service. It may be that direct mail or advertising is the primary initial vehicle, but in most situations, a combination of three or more approaches are necessary to maximize results.

3. Seek to construct an integrated program.

Determine how much each of your efforts is costing and how well each is working. The only way you can fine-tune your efforts is to determine which approaches are producing the best results for you. If you are using direct mail, you need to keep track of which lists produce what response rates. Ideally, you can come up with a number for your cost per customer obtained or sale made for various communication efforts. Note the start of the Wall Street Games marketing plan (see Exhibit 8–2, page 205), which points to a goal of "17,500 students with a $20 acquisition cost giving WSG a contribution to overhead of $400,000." In other words, it is expected that it will cost $20 in communication-related costs to obtain each student customer.

4. Monitor your results.

Beyond monitoring your results, you should be seeking out as much data as possible about individuals who respond to your communication efforts. What exactly are they buying? What are their business duties or their product preferences? The questions, of course, should be geared

5. Collect information aggressively.

8

Communicating with Your Market

toward whatever your company's particular information needs are. As pointed out earlier, you need systems and approaches for capturing and tabulating the information, so it can be used to advantage later.

Your communication approach needs to be described fully in the marketing plan. Ideally, support your plan by listing both the pros and cons of each technique. Also, you should provide budgetary justification for each one, which is the subject of the next chapter.

▶ **Exercises**

1. Describe within each of the following categories the two most important types or components of information essential for you to communicate to your marketplace:

    • Benefits information.

    • Product/service information.

    • Sales information.

    • Prospect/customer information.

2. What is your overall approach for using this information to communicate with your marketplace? What information will you emphasize and how will you communicate it?

3. Prioritize and discuss each of the key communication options you plan to use. Explain the pros and cons associated with each one and why you think the advantages outweigh the disadvantages.

4. List and discuss at least two unconventional approaches for communicating with your market. Describe advantages associated with each approach compared with conventional approaches.

5. Describe at least one approach to micromarketing that your company could take as part of fostering an ongoing relationship with customers and prospects.

(Worksheets for this chapter are provided on page 291)

8

Communicating
with Your Market

EXHIBIT 8–1

CUSTOMER INFORMATION

SMELL: FOLLOW YOUR NOSE

SMELL IN HISTORY

Smell has played a major role in history. Fragrances were used lavishly by whoever could afford them throughout the ancient world. Bodies, hair and clothes were all scented—but that was only the beginning. Beds, walls, tiles, chairs, and even the sails of ships were drenched in perfume. Mosques have been built with musk-infused cement.

Fragrances are associated with religion, magic, pleasure, healing and therapy throughout history. Written records of the use of fragrances stretch back over 3,000 years. The Assyrian Book of Herbs, written around 2,000 BC, contains recipes for medicinal herb mixtures and for fragrant oils and perfumes, including a scented drink to combat bad breath.

It was discovered that the sweet smells of flowers, herbs, and resins were enhanced if burned: hence the derivation of the word perfume—per fumum means "through smoke" in Latin.

• The Greeks claimed that the goddess Aphorodite invented perfume. In Ancient Greece, at special feasts, doves were soaked in perfume and sent flying over the heads of guests to sprinkle those below.

• When Napoleon was about to return to Paris from a campaign, he would write to Josephine telling her not to wash. . . He preferred her own 'natural' smell.

• Marie Antoinette adored fragrances, especially floral ones. In a time when the population never bathed, wearing perfume implied wealth and status (besides masking extreme body odour).

• Essential oils were used for their powerful antiseptic properties by the Egyptians to arrest the putrefaction of corpses. *continued*

EXHIBIT 8–1

continued

THE BODY SHOP

DESIGNER SMELLS

The perfume industry today is a multi-billion pound gamble. Dozens of new scents are launched every year—but few succeed. That's why the industry spends vast amounts of money on promotion and marketing.

A designer label often guarantees a new perfume arrives with a ready-made public profile. There are many people who want to buy a scent with a designer's name on it, even though it is accompanied by layers of expensive, wasteful packaging, and is marketed and hyped to the limit. Investigations indicate that often we smell with our eyes! Put certain scents in different bottles and we believe we smell what we see—hence the argument for the precious looking packaging.

But many others prefer to follow The Body Shop route.

• Our perfumes do not contain animal extracts, even if the name implies animals are involved—White Musk, for example. Wherever this is the case, we use suitable alternative ingredients—accurately matched to the original scent.

• Our perfume oils are very concentrated. Only a small amount is needed for each application.

• We prefer to let the product do the advertising and keep the packaging to a minimum. We don't make our customers pay for an image, for a name, for excessive packaging and glitzy bottles. We want to keep our perfumes economical to buy and use.

A perfume oil is sold in a small plastic bottle, or a simple glass one. The most popular perfume oils are available in non-aerosol eau de toilette pump sprays (containing alcohol to enable the perfume essences to vaporize easily).

continued

8

Communicating with Your Market

ALERT YOUR SENSE OF SMELL

The Body Shop Perfume Tester Bar is the place to sniff and dab. Try the wide selection of perfumes at your leisure—no one will take aim at you with a vapour spray. They are based on natural essential oils and range from fresh, fruity or flowery fragrances to woody or musky scents. Try several. Select different oils for different occasions or moods.

When testing perfumes, your nose can only cope with about six fragrances—one after the other. Leave at least 30 seconds, preferably 1–2 minutes, between smells.

Where to dab. . .

Apply a perfume wherever you like! Coco Chanel once said that perfume should be worn wherever you want to be kissed.

Start with pulse points at the neck, wrists and elbows. Once it was thought these areas were effective because they were warmer than the rest of the body. Not so. Recent research shows the variation in temperature is too small to make a difference. However, pulse points are among the most erogenous zones on the body.

YOUR OWN SMELL

A perfume does not smell the same on everyone—equally one scent will even vary at different times on the same person. Your skin colour and type affect a perfume's performance. Acidity and oiliness are key factors: the oilier the skin, the richer and more long-lasting the fragrance will be. Diet is also important: spices and garlic can emerge through the skin hours after a meal and affect the skin's chemistry for days. And be aware that other products you use (shampoo, hairspray) leave their own fragrance too, which can affect your perfume.

FROM THE MARKETING PLAN OF ★WALL STREET GAMES★

EXHIBIT 8-2

FOURTH ANNUAL
AT&T COLLEGIATE INVESTMENT CHALLENGE

OVERVIEW

The Fourth Annual AT&T Collegiate Investment Challenge planning and preparation has been in effect since early April, three months ahead of previous years marketing efforts. **This year's sales goal is 17,500 students with a $20 acquisition cost giving WSG a contribution to overhead of $400,000.** To reach this goal the marketing plan has been built around two specific objectives: To create a more effective and creative message than last year and to achieve a greater penetration and awareness on the campus.

The concept of the Collegiate Challenge, a fun and educational method to involve the students with Wall Street, seems in the past to have sold itself. After polling students and professors, prior creative efforts have been perceived as AT&T image advertising and not an effective Collegiate Investment Challenge message. In response to the creative message needed to sell this product WSG has teamed with American Passage (a collegiate direct selling specialist), and our own in-house ad agency to bring the message to a new creative level. The result, after weeks of discussion and preliminary designs, is a significant improvement. The marketing team feels that this new creative effort has effectively fulfilled the first priority of the marketing plan: **An effective message**.

The second part of the marketing plan objective is widespread penetration and awareness. Additional feedback on the program, from many students and professors surveyed, has pointed out a significant lack of awareness on campus of the Challenge. The Competition is both a product, as well as a promotion. The product itself is proven, but to sell the

continued

product, a successful promotional campaign is needed. This program includes registration deadlines, consistent creative messages, limited participation (currently limited to 20,000 participants), free premium offers (a Wall Street poster) and intense material distribution. The fourth annual plan includes the use of American Passage to help with this penetration as well as an over 100% increase in the WSG on-campus sponsor program.

American Passage has representatives on over 1,000 campuses in the United States. By using this rep system WSG will be able to distribute over 110,000 posters, 2,000,000 brochures, 500,000 flyers as well as display advertising in class directories and newspaper racks. This effort is both a combination of American Passage's mass distribution reps, as well as WSG's 800 reps who are more targeted to pre-qualified professors, business clubs and organizations. Working together the marketing team has effectively instituted the second objective of the marketing plan: **Widespread penetration and awareness.**

Although the proposed marketing plan has almost tripled the amount of materials distributed and quadrupled the number of campuses reached, the proposed increased expense is only 27%. The Third Annual Challenge expense was $276,000, as compared to the current marketing budget of $350,000 this year. This minimal increase is mostly due to volume discounts. Costs drop exponentially with the larger volumes of marketing materials printed. The small percentage increase in expenses can be attributed to the current recession and the state of the advertising industry. With deals that double our exposure, proposed advertising costs have remained similar to prior years.

Attached is the final marketing plan complete with sources, estimated sales, estimated cost and cost per sale (see Exhibit 2). Estimated sales

EXHIBIT 8-2
continued

★ WALL STREET GAMES ★

have been projected to have a marketing cost per unit of approximately $20, which is conservative, considering the large increase in marketing penetration. The largest contributor to sales (67%) is the group sales category which consists of the WSG on-campus sponsor and professor program, as well as the large distribution of American Passage. The college marketing plan has always been weighed heavily in this category, including the first year, and it has consistently contributed over 50% of the entire program. WSG has historically done exceptionally well in making positive alliances with many professors and business clubs across the country.

A third priority of the marketing plan, being worked on extensively over the summer, is to solidify more of these on-campus sponsor relationships. This objective is currently being achieved with an extensive "WSG broker" territorial rep program. Six WSG brokers have split the country into territories and concentrated their efforts to interview and enlist the best on-campus sponsors available (unlike prior years when any person on a campus was good enough). They are concentrating their efforts on business clubs and professors in order to provide us a permanent contact at a campus. The process will continue once the proposed updated on-campus file is completed. In prior years WSG had no way to track past contacts or sales from a certain school, making the sales effort for each year completely new. Proposed is a system that will cumulatively track contacts and sales information, and allow us to renew the successful sponsors (and drop unsuccessful sponsors) for future years.

THE MARKETING BUDGET

Measuring Results

I n this section of the market planning process, the proverbial rubber meets the road. How much will those wonderful strategies and tactics you've devised cost? How much revenue can you expect them to produce? Which approaches work best?

It is also the part of the plan where many executives run into trouble. They aren't sure how detailed or precise they should get or what purpose budgeting serves. As a consequence, they often don't do it, preferring instead to take a "global" view—and simply go with the plan to this point, measuring its success by the amount company revenues exceed costs.

The concerns are legitimate and the response understandable. It's tough enough to motivate yourself to do the parts of a plan when you understand the expectations and reasons behind them. But who needs fuzzy number-crunching exercises?

As noted at the start of the last chapter, however, the greatest strategies in the world do little to help a company if they aren't properly put into effect. A key part of the implementation process is developing a workable budget that guides spending and sets revenue expectations. As I pointed out in the last chapter, there are many tempting choices for advertising, public relations, direct-mail, and other marketing-related services. Without a clear budget, your costs can easily skyrocket and revenue expectations blur.

This chapter provides an overview of a marketing budget—obstacles you may encounter, the benefits a budget provides, and the tasks associated with developing your budget. Then it moves on to examine the experiences of Wall Street Games, which has done an excellent job of developing marketing budgets for its service lines.

The Marketing Budget and Process

As you are no doubt aware, a budget is a schedule of spending estimates tied to a specific allocation of revenues. Thus, a marketing budget begins with an itemization of expected expenditures on such items as display advertising, public relations services, postage for direct mail, production of informational brochures, and salaries or commissions to salespeople—all designed to achieve the plan's strategic goals. The expenditures are tied to an allocation of company funds appropriate to fund the program and yield attractive margins.

9

The Marketing Budget

If only life were that simple. In reality, there are three problems that come up when putting together a marketing budget:

1. Conflicting views on expenditures.

Many enticing options are available for carrying out the marketing plan. There are no end of magazines eager to sell advertising space, PR firms anxious to sell their services, and list brokers eager to rent you mailing lists. Moreover, many executives have biases when selecting among marketing implementation options. Some favor advertising, some lean toward direct mail, and others prefer the trade show route. These biases are usually based on successes the executives have achieved in the past using one or more approaches.

2. Uncertain revenues.

When it comes to such operating areas as manufacturing, research and development, engineering, and accounting, executives' tendencies are to view them as cost centers, with no direct responsibility for creating revenues. Therefore, in budgeting, these and other areas are allocated specific amounts of funding each year, based partly on their expected needs and on how the company is performing and what the area received the previous year.

The marketing function is often viewed differently, however. It is rightfully associated with producing revenues. How much revenues? Well, no one can say for certain because budgets deal with the future. So if the marketing program's revenues are uncertain, how can one decide what allocation to make? It's a chicken-and-egg-type dilemma.

Unlike conventional financial statements, such as profit-and-loss and cash-flow statements, there is no accepted format for a marketing budget. Executives often are uncertain how to set it up in terms of such things as the categories, the level of detail, and the inclusion of overhead expenses.

Executives also have varying expectations about how they should go about putting together a marketing budget. If one person writes the plan, should that person develop a budget as well? Or should the budgeting process be opened up to others in the marketing arena or to all executives in the company?

The three difficulties just described inhibit development of detailed marketing budgets in many companies. What these difficulties really suggest, though, is that as much as a marketing budget is a set of expenditure categories, it is also the result of a complex process. It is not a static financial process, but an active development one.

To put together a successful marketing budget requires give and take among marketing executives. In companies that place a high value on having a marketing budget, there is considerable discussion, debate, and negotiation. "We have extensive planning meetings, over a period of weeks, to hammer out our budget," says Steve Juedes, director of marketing at CareerTrack.

Nor is the process ever truly completed. "We adjust the budget by the quarter. We use the previous quarter's budget to make adjustments. The budgeting is really part of a dynamic process."

3. Unclear format and procedures.

The Marketing Budget

9

What Good Is a Marketing Budget?

Because many companies do quite well with marketing plans that don't include a marketing budget, one can reasonably question its need. But then, one can point to various companies that do well without a written business or marketing plan of any type.

I answer these objections on two levels. The business climate has become so uncertain and competition so intense that frequent improvements and fine-tuning of strategies and tactics are necessary. Without a written plan that includes a record of expected expenditures and revenues, making rational changes becomes difficult. How can you determine the impact of a change from display advertising to direct mail if you don't know the financial performance of your original plan?

From a strategic perspective, failure to do a marketing budget has an opportunity cost. Companies without a marketing budget lose out on important advantages. The four principal benefits of a marketing budget are:

1. Protection from unexpected developments.

One certainty in business is that not everything will proceed according to plan. As careful and well thought out as your marketing plan may be, you can be sure that some of your approaches won't work. Hopefully, some will work out much better than expected.

With a budget, though, it is easy to determine quickly disparities between expectations and reality and do something about the situation. If one approach isn't working and another is coming in above expectations, you can shift expenditures to more of the good stuff.

Most important, a marketing budget affords protection against continuing to do the wrong thing for too long. You can easily waste valuable resources and time pursuing misguided strategies and tactics. By comparing results to budget, you can change course in your company before a small error in judgment becomes serious hemorrhaging.

Over a period of years, putting together a marketing budget enables you to predict ever more confidently the effects of your marketing strategies and tactics. By monitoring how your budget compares with reality, you can see where your projections were misguided and identify trends helpful in establishing budgets for the future. For example, you may find that direct-mail efforts are yielding slowly declining revenues, while expenditures associated with trade show displays are showing minor improvements. Identifying such a trend may well prompt you to search out additional trade shows and obtain consulting services on improving your displays. Instead of scrambling to figure out why revenues are declining, your company could be continuing on the growth curve.

2. Project the future.

Putting together a marketing budget is tedious, because it forces everyone involved to become specific about their spending and expectations. It often yields surprises for those involved in the process. For example, the total costs associated with direct mail or trade shows are often much higher than individuals realize, once all the

3. Introduce discipline into the organization.

9

The Marketing Budget

expenses are quantified. By getting estimates in advance and anticipating all the costs, an organization has a clear picture of the commitments it's making.

4. Measure marketing effectiveness.

There should also be a focus on whether the expenditures will yield an appropriate payback. For direct mail, you are likely seeking a direct dollar-for-dollar payback plus an additional amount to cover overhead and profit. But if your company has hired a public relations firm to arrange speaking engagements for its top executives, you may be more interested in enabling the company to become known and respected in its industry, which your sales force can exploit over the next two or three years. The immediate payback won't be easy to quantify, but at least that will be understood in advance.

Indeed, a marketing budget should serve the additional purpose of focusing everyone in the marketing department on common goals and expectations. Those involved in public relations or trade shows know exactly what they have to work with and what results are expected.

If the budget is well thought out and referred to regularly, it can work wonders in focusing an organization on common goals.

Developing Your Budget

Putting together a marketing budget forces a company to quantify all the planning that has occurred up until now. If exploited to its fullest, the process enables a company to give final form to its overall marketing plan. Among the tasks to be completed are:

You know what your strategy is with regard to your target market, position, and competition, and you have identified approaches for conveying key information. At this point, you should establish clear priorities.

1. Set priorities.

One useful approach is to ask which implementation activity you would choose if you could afford only one. In other words, if you were in the situation described by Ken Meyers in the last chapter, with barely enough money for one type of information-related activity, what would it be? If you could afford only two, what would the second be? And so on.

Another consideration: If your top activity turns out to cost more than you expect—as Meyers's efforts on the advertising front did—what will you do that will cost less?

Where will the money come from to pay for the marketing activities? Ideally, your answer will be guided by your company's past marketing experiences. Here is where you see the incremental, or long-term value, of a marketing budget. If you know what you spent in previous years and what results you achieved, the answer becomes easier to

2. Determine the marketing allocation.

The Marketing Budget

9

determine than if you are budgeting for the first time.

If your established company is doing a marketing budget for the first time, you will need to do some research to uncover what was spent in the past. You should also try to correlate results with the past activities. How many customers came in as a result of a particular advertising or direct-mail campaign? How many prospects did you obtain from a trade show, and what percentage of those were converted into customers?

If you are in a start-up situation or are unable to determine what was spent in the past, investigate how much companies in comparable businesses spend. Sometimes, industry trade groups can provide data showing that companies spend some average amount, like 10% or 15% of total revenues on marketing. Such figures are best used for guidance rather than as absolute numbers.

3. Investigate costs.

It's easy to underestimate what different marketing activities cost, as Ken Meyers discovered when he sought an advertising program with a $100,000 budget. Ideally, you should have enough information to do some rough estimates at the time you are setting priorities and estimating revenues.

But you will have to do additional investigation after establishing priorities, as various approaches can change over time and new techniques come into play. For instance, the recession of the early 1990s caused many magazines, newspapers, and television stations to lower their rates or negotiate discounted rates, even if their published rates didn't change. Many newspapers also opened their pages to inexpensive flyers to lower promotional costs.

An important part of the budgeting process is setting ground rules for how you will do things and what you expect to happen. Continuing on a point raised at the end of Chapter 8, will you do your public relations in-house or will you hire outsiders? If you do it in-house, how do you budget, especially if the people doing the public relations are also tending to other duties? You may elect to consider them part of general and administrative, or you may want to quantify the time they each spend on a particular product or service and include as an expense their proportionate salaries and benefits. You may also want to determine how to calculate and apportion overhead—rent, telephones, secretaries, etc.

4. Establish guidelines.

Another important issue is establishing expectations for various activities. Aside from what you may have accomplished in the past, what are your expectations for activities now being planned? Do you want to establish minimum goals for number of inquiries or amount of revenues generated from particular activities? How long will you give employees to achieve their goals? One quarter or one year?

Tim DeMello of Wall Street Games cautions that in establishing expectations, it is important to distinguish between goals and plans. "Our goals are more of a wish list

9

The Marketing Budget

kind of thing. Our plans are what we feel we can achieve. In our budgets we try to concentrate on plans. We want to do things we can substantiate."

The Wall Street Games Approach

A case study helps give form to the questions raised in this chapter. As noted, there is no one right way to develop a marketing budget. But Wall Street Games has done an excellent job of developing its own budget approach and format. Its three principal budget tables covering its Fourth Annual AT&T Collegiate Investment Challenge are reproduced in Exhibit 9–2, page 231. They begin with a statement of expected revenues and one of expected costs. (For a summary explanation, see Exhibit 8–2.) Here is how Wall Street Games approaches its budget tables:

• Set overall expectations.

DeMello and his two vice-presidents establish the company's overall marketing and implementation strategy for the year. Two key categories of projected data come out of their planning: the G&A, or overhead, amount and the expected "contribution" of each of the company's two main divisions.

For G&A, the real question, says DeMello, is, "How much does it cost to have the resources available to the marketing people? These resources are basically three departments—MIS, operations/finance, and in-house advertising and communications." And, of course, there are rent, utilities, and related expenses associated with keeping them operating.

Contribution is the net of revenues less cost of goods sold (contest packages, monthly statements, phone time, phone operator salaries), leaving gross profit. From that the company subtracts variable costs associated with selling, including advertising, direct mail, brochures, and monthly statements to customers. What is left is the contribution, which is used to offset the company's overhead. The amount by which all the contributions exceed overhead, of course, is the company's profit.

In many companies, sales costs are lumped together with G&A. By pulling sales costs out, Wall Street Games can monitor the efficiency of its marketing budgets and easily determine how each individual program performs. This approach is useful for any company with more than one product or service line.

DeMello and his officers estimate overall G&A along with the contribution expected from each of the company's two main divisions, investments and sports. Investments' contribution comes from five events and sports' from six events.

But the Wall Street Games officials don't just come up with three numbers. Instead, they come up with nine, based on three potential outcomes: plan, goal, and minimum requirement.

The plan numbers are what the company realistically hopes to achieve. The goals are what the company believes could be achieved if everything goes according to the most optimistic assumptions. And the minimum requirements are the opposite of the goals—the amounts realized in a worst-case scenario. The table in Exhibit 9–1, page 230, shows the company's projections for 1992, made in the fall of 1991.

• Focus on contribution.

Once those parameters are established, the vice-president of each division plans the individual division events to meet the targets. These events are contests among participants to determine, in Investment Division events, who performs best in selecting and managing a stock portfolio and, in Sports Division events, who picks winning teams. According to DeMello, "We are looking for a contribution of between $100,000 and $700,000 for each event, depending on the event. We have bought them the divisions' resources like MIS, office space, employee salaries, and so forth. But all the variable costs come out of their event budgets—advertising, direct mail, and cash prizes."

One event I examine, the Collegiate Investment Challenge, is intended to provide a contribution to overhead of $400,000. The other four events handled by the Investment Division must be similarly planned to meet the total numbers in column one of the table in Exhibit 9–1.

• Allocate the budget.

Of course, the numbers arrived at for contribution can't just be approximations or rough expectations for each division. Four months before each event, the half-dozen or so individuals involved in various aspects of marketing for the Investment Division sit down to hammer out spending targets and expectations.

There are a number of categories, corresponding with the target markets and the information/selling sources to be used. The two target markets are college students/faculty and high school students. Wall Street Games relies primarily on sponsor involvement, magazine advertising, campus selling efforts, and public relations to inform and reach each target market. (See the second table in Exhibit 9–2, page 233.)

The allocations just described should be done as rationally as possible. The most rational approach is to examine how well each approach worked in the past.

The first column in the second table of Exhibit 9–2 shows actual sales for a number of approaches used in the last Collegiate Investment Challenge. For instance, ads in *U Magazine* resulted in 603 sales. Based on that result and the expectation that the upcoming ads are an improvement over the previous ones, the budget estimates that the new ad will pull 800 sales.

Of course, not all approaches will have the benefit of past experience guiding the projections. It could be that a particular advertising outlet or promotional vehicle is being tried for the first time. Or if it was tried before, perhaps no follow-up was done to assess the results.

In such situations, the estimating process becomes more difficult. You can examine your results from similar techniques you have tried; for example, Wall Street Games uses its results from *U Magazine* to estimate other adver-

• **Establish realistic revenue goals.**

The Marketing Budget

tising outlets. You can obtain intelligence on how approaches have worked for others who have tried what you are considering—from executives of noncompeting companies in similar industries or companies in your industry located in other regions. But basically, you are reduced to estimating potential results for each technique.

• Determine costs.

Once again, the more detail you can obtain, the more accurate your budget will be. The second table in Exhibit 9–2 shows under "Est. Budget" how much each activity is expected to cost. Two ads in *U Magazine*, for instance, cost $25,000. Having 800 campus reps costs $61,201. Some of the efforts, such as those from *USA Today* and AT&T, have only minimal costs attached because they are sponsors and underwrite the advertising expenses, leaving only some production costs.

The third table in Exhibit 9–2, page 235, "Estimated Marketing Budget," breaks down each estimated cost into its components as necessary. Thus, the expenses associated with the 800 campus reps are based mainly on a number of mailings and follow-up letters to past customers and new prospects. There are costs associated with letterhead, #10 envelopes to mail promotional packages to prospects, #9 envelopes for the prospects to return the forms, and list rentals, as well as payments to the reps. By breaking the mailing costs down on a per-piece or per-name basis, the company can easily compare costs of paper and list rentals.

By itemizing all the costs, the company's marketing

officials can feel confident they will not confront unpleasant surprises as they proceed.

Wall Street Games' officials must also see to it that the budget is implemented in a timely way—that the direct-mail promotions are sent, the advertisements placed, and similar tasks completed to reach prospects at the most opportune time to influence buying decisions. Moreover, the company needs to be geared up to handle the uneven customer flow. "If you run a TV ad and 200 calls come in and you can't handle them, you aren't helping yourself," says DeMello. "It's better to have 50 calls. Or, if you are ready for 200 calls from an ad at 7:30, what do you do with all the extra phone operators who are waiting until the next ad comes on at 10:30?"

• Time the budget.

To help in planning its timing, the company's marketing plan includes assignment sheets detailing who is responsible for various tasks, such as obtaining envelopes, stationery, and a cash-flow sheet displaying when expenditures are expected to be made. All employees in the marketing area know exactly what is expected of them.

At the end of the written marketing plan is a place for the key people involved in planning the budget to sign off. The Investment Division's manager signs the plan as the preparer and the Investment Division vice-president signs in approval. Then the various department heads responsible for supporting the process—MIS, finance, operations—

• Get "ownership."

The Marketing Budget

affix their signatures. And finally, Tim DeMello and his counterpart on the company's management team provide approvals. Salaries, bonuses, and overall advancement are tied to meeting or beating the budgeted contribution to overhead. Many people's future in the company are thus linked to the budget's viability.

• **Figure productivity.**

The most important data to come out of a marketing budget emerges after the money has been spent—when results are analyzed. Ideally, it is when executives measure the performance, or productivity, of their marketing budgets. Marketing productivity is the cost per customer acquired. It can be calculated only after the budget has been implemented and results are known in terms of business generated.

Marketing productivity is easiest to calculate in businesses dependent on direct mail or retailing, in which results are usually apparent within a fairly short time. In the second table of Exhibit 9–2, the column after "Source of Sales" is for "Ext." This is a special extension number contained in each ad, brochure, PR release, and other promotional material that enables the company to correlate telephone responses with the marketing approach used. Thus, ads in *USA Today* provide the company's 800 number plus Ext. 26; *Black Collegiate* ads show Ext. 27, and so forth.

In businesses with long selling periods, such as for legal and consulting services, or for big-ticket capital goods, marketing productivity is usually more difficult to calculate. In such businesses, prospects may take six months, a year, or longer to become customers. After such a long period, it may not be certain whether they made their commitments based on a particular ad, an in-house newsletter, a sales call, follow-up telemarketing, or some combination of these approaches. (For guidance on measuring marketing productivity in these situations, see the box on page 227.)

Tim DeMello measures marketing productivity by calculating the total cost of a marketing activity and dividing it by the number of customer acquisitions. A telemarketing campaign that costs $100,000 and yields 5,000 sales costs $20 per acquisition. In the second table of Exhibit 9–2, the estimated cost per sale of each marketing approach has been calculated. However, these are only estimates; DeMello knows from hard experience that the real numbers vary widely. Here is one past outcome from a Collegiate Investment Challenge (college only) that he describes in chart form (derived from Exhibit 9–2):

MARKETING APPROACH	# UNITS SOLD	COST/ACQUISITION
Database	500	$10.71
Sponsors	505	7.21
Direct marketing	1,835	26.82
Group sales	11,550	22.12
Public relations	800	4.62
Total	15,190	$20.89 (AVERAGE)

Not surprisingly, DeMello would like to smooth out the wide variations in the cost per acquisition among the approaches used. Within the direct-marketing category, some mailing lists result in costs of $40 or more per acquisition, while others are in the $10 to $15 range. "We need to get smarter," he observes. "If we could cut out the high-cost acquisitions, we'd do a lot better overall."

But beyond analyzing the mailing lists, the company is striving constantly to measure its results and apply them to future projections. "Some of our biggest mistakes have come from trying to go too far—trying to find new sources that will generate orders. Our total orders may increase, but too often, the cost per acquisition shoots up."

That concern caused DeMello to push the Investment Division to strive for 17,500 student participants, at a projected $20 per acquisition cost, rather than 20,000 participants at a possibly significantly higher acquisition cost (see Exhibit 8–2, page 205). "The cost of getting the extra 2,500 rises," he notes. He wasn't certain by how much it would rise, but he had enough experience to know he didn't want to take the risk.

Why doesn't Wall Street Games simply focus on those activities with the greatest productivity and discard the costly ones? Because the high-productivity approaches are being used to their maximum. The company is using as much of the promotional activities from its sponsors as it can. In order to keep growing, the company must scout out and expand additional approaches.

Measuring the Unmeasurable

Wall Street Games can easily determine what marketing tactic stimulated a prospect or customer to call its 800 number by assigning different extension numbers to its direct-mail and advertising programs.

But for many types of companies, such as those that market products or services with long selling cycles—capital goods or complex consulting services—it is often difficult to learn precisely what marketing action helped make the sale. Perhaps there was an article quoting an executive of a company six months earlier that a prospect saved. Or a newsletter a company distributes to prospects and clients rang a bell. Or maybe a prospect saw a company executive give a presentation at a trade show.

There is no magic way of solving this dilemma, but there are ways to get a handle on measuring the effectiveness of marketing actions, including:

1. Ask prospects how they found you. Instruct all those who deal with prospects, including receptionists and secretaries, to inquire of everyone who seeks information about your company how they learned about you. Not everyone will know precisely because, in many cases, they learned about your organization from a number of sources.

2. Capture the information. Keep a database of all prospects, including the information about how they learned about your firm.

3. Try at least some marketing approaches that lend themselves to measurement. Even if you sell a complex product or service, you can publish a newsletter or run an ad in industry publications. Experiment with a coupon or bingo card that individuals can return seeking more information. Keep track of which lists or publications generated the responses.

4. Monitor your "sales cycle." This is the amount of time from when someone first expresses interest in your company's product or service until you close the sale. This can further guide you as to which approaches bring in the best prospects.

Moreover, the company is obtaining its cost-per-acquisition data after the fact. And as it grows, it must continually test new techniques. If acquisition costs are higher than expected, executives must question the source of the problem. Was the mailing list inappropriate? Was the ad copy off-target? As DeMello notes, "For us, print advertising works best, but we need to keep trying new approaches for when print gets tired."

A Systematic Process

Wall Street Games does a great job of budgeting, but you should keep in mind that there is more than one way to create a budget. Its budget works because it has been customized to the company's highly specific needs in the areas of direct-mail, advertising, and on-campus promotion. But the Wall Street Games approach also works because it is based on a systematic planning process that involves the following key components:

1. Budget separately for each product or service line.
2. Set specific financial targets.
3. Determine the spending necessary to meet the targets.
4. Evaluate the plan's outcome.
5. Use the results to improve the process the next time around.

▶ **Exercises**

Begin putting together a marketing budget for your company.
Go through the following exercises as needed:

1.   List the people who will work on the marketing budget.

2.   List the marketing information and communication priorities for each
     of your company's products/services for the next year to reach your
     target market and carry out your marketing strategy.

3.   Determine how much you are prepared to spend on marketing activities.

4.   Calculate how much each of the activities listed in your priorities will
     cost to carry out.

5.   Estimate the revenues you can expect to obtain from each activity.

6.   Estimate the marketing productivity associated with each activity.

7.   Revise your allocation and cost estimates as necessary to achieve
     your goals.

8.   Determine what approaches you will use to measure results from
     each activity.

9.   Establish a timetable for implementing your budget.

(Worksheets for this chapter are provided on page 296)

The Marketing Budget

9

FROM THE MARKETING PLAN OF
★WALL STREET GAMES★

EXHIBIT 9-1

WALL STREET GAMES
PROJECTED 1992 CONTRIBUTION AND G&A

1992	Contrib./Invest. Division	Contrib./Sports Division	G&A	Oper. Profit Potential
Plan	$1.2	$1.6	$1.8	$1.0
Goal	$1.5	$1.9	$1.7	$1.7
Min. req.	$.7	$1.0	$1.7	Break Even

($ in millions)

EXHIBIT 9–2

COLLEGIATE INVESTMENT CHALLENGE

FROM THE MARKETING PLAN OF ★WALL STREET GAMES★

PRODUCT MANAGERS REPORT
As of 7/31/91

	3rd Annual (Actual) Gross $	Per Unit	4th Annual (Estimated) Gross $	Per Unit	Variance Variance $	Variance per Unit	4th Annual (Plan) Gross $	Per Unit
Units Sold	13,397		17,500		4,103		17,500	
1. EVENT CONTRIBUTION REVENUES								
Registration Fees	$669,164	$49.95	$874,125	$49.95	$204,961	$0.00	$834,124	$47.66
Shipping/Handling	$60,846	$4.54	$96,950	$5.54	$36,104	$1.00	$58,976	$3.37
Refunds	($23,725)	($1.77)	($35,000)	($2.00)	($11,275)	($0.23)	($20,852)	($1.19)
Declines/Outstanding	($9,000)	($0.67)	($11,725)	($0.67)	($2,725)	($0.00)		
TOTAL NET REVENUES	$697,285	$52.05	$924,350	$52.82	$227,065	$0.77	$872,248	$49.84
COSTS OF ACQUISITION								
Marketing Expense	($276,504)	($20.64)	($350,000)	($20.00)	($73,496)	$0.64	($257,200)	$14.70
Sales discounts			($27,450)	($1.57)	($27,450)	($1.57)	($8,340)	($0.48)
TOTAL COSTS OF ACQUIS	($276,504)	($20.64)	($377,450)	($21.57)	($100,946)	($0.93)	($265,540)	($15.17)
PRELIMINARY EVENT CONTRIBUTION	$420,781	$31.41	$546,900	$31.25	$126,119	($0.16)	$606,708	$34.67
COST OF SALES—VARIABLE								
Contest Packages	($21,130)	($1.58)	($27,650)	($1.58)	($6,520)	($0.00)	($28,000)	($1.60)
Credit Card Fees	($13,564)	($1.01)	($17,675)	($1.01)	($4,111)	$0.00	($18,756)	($1.07)
Monthly Statements	($79,836)	($5.96)	($96,250)	($5.50)	($16,414)	$0.46	($100,800)	($5.76)

continued

The Marketing Budget

9

PRODUCT MANAGER'S REPORT

EXHIBIT 9–2

COLLEGIATE INVESTMENT CHALLENGE
continued

	3rd Annual (Actual) Gross $	Per Unit	4th Annual (Estimated) Gross $	Per Unit	Variance Variance $	per Unit	4th Annual (Plan) Gross $	Per Unit
Shipping Expense	($39,890)	($2.98)	($65,275)	($3.73)	($25,385)	($0.75)	($34,476)	($1.97)
Broker Allocation	($46,629)	($3.48)	($60,900)	($3.48)	($14,271)	$0.00	($71,000)	($4.06)
Phone Allocation	($51,162)	($3.82)	($66,850)	($3.82)	($15,688)	($0.00)	($63,100)	($3.61)
TOTAL VAR. COST	($252,211)	($18.83)	($334,600)	($19.12)	($82,389)	($0.29)	($316,132)	($18.06)
VARIABLE EVENT CONTRIBUTION	$168,570	$12.58	$212,300	$12.13	$43,730	($0.45)	$290,576	$16.60
2) Advertising & Information Revenues								
900 Lines Revenues	$32,642	$2.44	$42,700	$2.44	$10,058	$0.00	$40,000	$2.29
Other Revenues			$4,375	$0.25	$4,375	$0.25	$2,000	$0.11
COST OF SALES								
900 Line Fees	($18,213)	($1.36)	($23,800)	($1.36)	($5,587)	($0.00)	($21,040)	($1.20)
Other	($4,979)	($0.37)	($8,750)	($0.50)	($3,771)	($0.13)	($12,000)	($0.69)
VARIABLE A&I CONTRIBUTION	$9,450	$0.54	$14,525	$0.83	$5,075	$0.29	$8,960	$0.51
NET CONTRIBUTION BEFO	$178,020	$10.17	$226,825	$12.96	$48,805	$2.79	$299,536	$17.12
FIXED REVENUES (costs)								
Sponsorship Fees	$157,673		$250,000		$92,327		$250,000	
Inventory Writeoff	($9,937)		($5,000)		$4,937		($5,000)	
Cash Prizes	($74,500)		($74,500)				($74,500)	
NET EVENT CONTRIBUTION	$261,193		$402,325		$141,132		$475,036	

★ WALL STREET GAME$ ★

COLLEGIATE INVESTMENT CHALLENGE
continued

SOURCES OF SALES, NOVEMBER 1, 1991–FEBRUARY 28, 1992
Selling Period: September 1, 1991–October 31, 1991

COLLEGE DIVISION

ACTUAL 90-91 SALES	SOURCE OF SALES	EXT	EST. SALES	EST. GROSS SALES	EST. BUDGET	SALES COMMISSION	DISCOUNT ALLOW	REFUND ALLOW	COST PER SALE	COST OF SALES	EST. CONTRIB.
	SPONSORS										
338	1. USA Today	26	400	$22,196	$0		$0	$599	$1.50	($18.29)	$14,281
	2. AT&T Rideboard	13	75	$4,162	$2,885		$0	$112	$39.97	($18.29)	($207)
	3. AT&T Newsletter	14	30	$1,665	$0		$0	$45	$1.50	($18.29)	$1,071
	TOTAL		505	$28,022	$2,885	$0	$0	$757	$7.21	($18.29)	$15,144
	DIRECT MARKETING										
603	1. Am. Pas (Dir. Class)	21	800	$44,392	$16,000		$0	$1,199	$21.50	($18.29)	$12,561
	2. U Magazine (2x)	22	800	$44,392	$25,000		$0	$1,199	$32.75	($18.29)	$3,561
	3. Campus Connections (2x)		100	$5,549	$0	$1,500	$0	$150	$16.50	($18.29)	$2,070
	4. Black Collegiate (1x)	27	50	$2,775	$2,716		$0	$75	$55.82	($18.29)	($931)
	5. Scorecard	28	35	$1,942	$1,250		$0	$52	$37.21	($18.29)	($0)
	6. The Leader	25	50	$2,775	$0		$0	$75	$1.50	($18.29)	$1,785
	SUBTOTAL		1,835	$101,824	$44,966	$1,500	0	$2,750	$26.82	($18.29)	$19,046
	WSG DATABASE										
488	1. Renewal	15	500	$27,745	$4,608		$0	$749	$10.71	($18.29)	$13,243
	GROUP SALES										
5,250	1. Campus Reps (800 reps)	10,12	5,200	$288,548	$61,201	$33,800	$0	$7,792	$19.77	($18.29)	$90,647
1,782	2. Professors	123	1,650	$91,559	$11,770		$0	$2,473	$8.63	($18.29)	$47,137
	3. Am. Pass (postering)	40	2,700	$149,823	$74,400		$0	$4,046	$29.05	($18.29)	$21,994
	4. Am. Pas. (Field oper.)		1,000	$55,490	$25,000		$0	$1,499	$26.50	($18.29)	$10,702
	5. Am. Pas. (Adrax)	80	1,000	$55,490	$32,001		$0	$1,499	$33.50	($18.29)	$3,700
	TOTAL		11,550	$640,910	$204,372	$33,800	$0	$17,308	$22.12	($18.29)	$174,180
	PUBLIC RELATIONS										
506	1. Friend	30	350	$19,422	$0		$0	$524	$1.50	($18.29)	$12,496
872	2. Other	40	450	$24,971	$2,500		$0	$674	$7.05	($18.29)	$13,566
	TOTAL		800	$44,392	$2,500	$0	$0	$1,199	$4.62	($18.29)	$26,061
	TOTALS		15,190	$842,893	$259,331	$35,300	$0	$22,762	$20.89	($18.29)	$247,674

Marketing
dget

9

EXHIBIT 9-2

★ WALL STREET GAMES ★

COLLEGIATE INVESTMENT CHALLENGE
continued

HIGH SCHOOLS

ACTUAL 90-91 SALES	SOURCE OF SALES	EXT	EST. SALES	EST. GROSS SALES	EST. BUDGET	SALES COMMISSION	DIS-COUNT ALLOW	REFUND ALLOW	COST PER SALE	COST OF SALES	EST. CONTRIB.
	SPONSORS										
85	1. USA Today	26	100	$5,549		$0	$1,000	$150	$11.50	($18.29)	$2,570
25	2. USA Today (Reps)	26	25	$1,387		$0	$250	$37	$11.50	($18.29)	$643
	TOTAL		125	$6,936		$0	$1,250	$187	$11.50	($18.29)	$3,213
	DIRECT MARKETING										
	Print Advertising										
	1. The Leader	25	50	$2,775		$0	$500	$75	$11.50	($18.29)	$1,285
	Target Lists										
	1. Broker Mailing		150	$8,324	$1,080		$1,500	$225	$18.70	($18.29)	$2,775
	WSG Database										
77	1. Renewal	15	100	$5,549	$1,728		$1,000	$150	$28.78	($18.29)	$842
	GROUP SALES										
1,562	1. Educators/FBLA	11	1,525	$84,622	$29,425		$15,250	$2,285	$30.79	($18.29)	$9,770
	PUBLIC RELATIONS										
77	1. Friend	30	100	$5,549	$0		$1,000	$150	$11.50	($18.29)	$2,570
	2. BRN		10	$555	$0		$100	$15	$11.50	($18.29)	$257
450	3. Other	40	250	$13,873	$2,500		$2,500	$375	$21.50	($18.29)	$3,925
	TOTAL		360	$19,976	$2,500	$0	$3,600	$539	$18.44	($18.29)	$6,753
	TOTALS		2,260	$125,407	34,733	$0	$22,600	$3,387	$26.87	($18.29)	$23,352
	Agency Fee				$10,000						($10,000)
	Premium Poster				$8,500						($8,500)
	Creative (Gilbert Scherer)				$5,500						($5,500)
	RESERVATIONS				$2,380						($2,380)
	TOTAL		17,450	$968,301	$320,444	$35,300	$22,600	$26,149	$23.18	($18.29)	$415,147
	GRAND TOTAL*			$355,744							

*Fixed Contribution of $170,500 included

234

EXHIBIT 9-2

WALL STREET GAMES

ESTIMATED MARKETING BUDGET
November 1, 1991 — February 28, 1992

COLLEGE

SPONSORS	PLACEMENT					TOTAL
1. USA TODAY						$0
2. AT&T Rideboard	$2,885					$2,885
3. AT&T Newsletter						$0

DIRECT MARKETING

Print Advertising	PLACEMENT					TOTAL
1. Am. Pass. (Dir. class)	$16,000					$16,000
2. U Magazine (2x)	$25,000					$25,000
3. Campus Connections (2x)	$0					$0
4. Black Collegiate	$2,716					$2,716
5. Scorecard	$1,250					$1,250
6. The Leader	$0					$0

WSG DATABASE	QUANTITY	MAILER	POSTAGE	LASER	STUFFING	TOTAL
1. RENEWAL	8,000	$0.19	$0.29	$0.05	$0.05	$4,608
- perf letthead 1	8.000	$0.04				
- #9 envelope 1	8,000	$0.02				
- brochure 1	8,000	$0.09				
- 9X12 envelope 1	8,000	$0.05				

GROUP SALES

1. On Campus Rep	QUANTITY	COST	POSTAGE			TOTAL
A. Renewal Mailing	150	$0.17	$0.29			$68
- nonperf letthead 1	150	$0.04				
-#10 envelope 1	150	$0.03				
-#9 envelope 1	150	$0.02				
-sponsor form 1	150	$0.04				
-flyer 1	150	$0.04				
	QUANTITY	COST	POSTAGE		STUFFING	TOTAL
B) New rep mailing 1	3,800	$0.17	$0.29		$0.05	$1,900
- nonperf letthead 1	3,800	$0.04				
- #10 envelope 1	3,800	$0.03				
- #9 envelope 1	3,800	$0.02				
- sponsor form 1	3,800	$0.04				
- flyer 1	3,800	$0.04				*continued*

9

The Marketing Budget

EXHIBIT 9–2

COLLEGIATE INVESTMENT CHALLENGE
continued

ESTIMATED MARKETING BUDGET
November 1, 1991 — February 28, 1992
continued

COLLEGE

SPONSORS	PLACEMENT					TOTAL
	QUANTITY	COST	LIST	POSTAGE	STUFFING	
C) Professor Mailing	11,500	$0.23	$0.10	$0.29	$.05	$7,590
- nonperf letthead	1	11,500	$0.04			
- #10 envelope	1	11,500	$0.03			
- #9 envelope	1	11,500	$0.02			
- sponsor form	1	11,500	$0.04			
- school form	2	23,000	$0.10			
	WAGES	BONUS	INCENTIVES			TOTAL
D) Broker Calling	1,600	$1,200	$2,000			$4,800
QUANTITY	COST	LIST	POSTAGE			TOTAL
E) Follow up letters	800	$0.07	$0.29			$284.00
- nonperf letthead 1	800	$0.04				
- #10 envelope 1	800	$0.03				
	800	$0.07	$0.29			$284.00
- nonperf letthead 1	800	$0.04				
- #10 envelope 1	800	$0.03				

TIMETABLES AND MANAGEMENT

It's All in the Details

I t wasn't a major setback in his company, but Tim DeMello recalls the incident like it was yesterday. Wall Street Games was due to mail out about 10,000 brochures via third-class mail for a Collegiate Investment Challenge.

Because third-class mail is delivered in one to three weeks, it must be prepared earlier than first-class mail, which takes two to five days. The advantage is that users of third-class mail pay between 30% and 60% of the first-class rate.

Unfortunately, Wall Street Games failed to meet its internal deadline for getting the pieces out to reach prospects before the scheduled challenge. That meant the company had to send the items out as first-class mail—at an additional cost of between $2,500 and $3,000 over projections. "So even if the mailing was as successful as projected, we lost some money," says DeMello.

Wall Street Games was actually lucky. I have seen situations in which the U.S. Postal Service rejected 5,000 or 10,000 pieces of direct mail because they failed to meet one of its strict regulations about address or stamp placement. The mistakes necessitated the purchase and printing of new envelopes to be restuffed and affixed with new address labels.

In DeMello's mind, strategy results from a combination of subjective factors—historical information, industry trends, and a gut feel of what will happen. Implementation, though, results from disciplined planning and scheduling. "It is unforgiving," he observes.

DeMello understands the dangers of failing to meet schedules. I'm referring not just to sending mail late or in the wrong form. There are other problems as well, such as not getting ads completed on time, not having displays ready for trade shows, and not delivering products when promised in your promotional literature.

The dangers associated with such failures are twofold: First, you risk wrecking your marketing budget. Second, and often more important, you risk losing marketing effectiveness. So you often wind up paying more and getting less in return. In this chapter I cover two principal areas: putting the budget into effect and developing systems to aid in future budgeting and planning.

Executing the Budget: Four Common Problems

For the uninitiated, it's difficult to anticipate how to execute a marketing budget. You'd think that once you have the money apportioned, it would simply be a matter of going out and spending it as directed. But there are invariably four types of problems that undermine the execution process:

For many types of products and services, there are optimal times for selling certain products. Some obvious examples are the Christmas season for toy and other retailers, the springtime for gardening equipment marketers, and the fall for seminar promoters. These businesses need to have the right inventory or services as well as complete their advertising, direct-mail, and other promotional campaigns so they reach consumers at the right time.

In some cases, the influences are more subtle. If you are testing a direct-mail list to determine which geographic area to focus a larger campaign on, you'll be unable to launch the second campaign until you've gotten the test results. That sounds obvious, but the impact on a company's scheduling can be profound. Time must be allowed to analyze the test effort and to obtain the new campaign's mailing lists, print the material, stuff envelopes, and affix labels—and still reach prospective customers at the optimum time.

Timing problems are common in new-product introductions—especially in the technology field. One is a failure to deliver new products when promised. As one example, a small distributor of Apple Macintosh components advertised a long-awaited new type of accelerator board in a magazine for Macintosh users. Dozens of Macintosh users phoned in their orders via the 800 number. Unfortunately, the manufacturer failed to deliver the accelerator boards when promised. The users who ordered the $200 item were told that the boards were expected in a few days. Days

1. Timing deficiencies.

10

Timetables and Management

turned into weeks, and still no boards. Both the distributor and the manufacturer eventually suffered—not only because many of the customers canceled their orders, but also because many of those customers were angry enough to swear off both the distributor and the manufacturer for future orders.

Executives too often fail to allow sufficient time to complete important tasks. Then they may face the choice that confronted Tim DeMello: Pay more to get the job done on time (via increased postage, labor, and other costs) or be late. Of course, if the timing is way off, no amount of money can correct the situation and customers become alienated.

2. Deadline problems.

No matter how long you think things will take, they will actually take much longer than expected. Executing the budget is in large measure meeting deadlines.

Too often deadlines get extended or ignored altogether. In some cases, tasks aren't completed in a coordinated way. Thus, most deadlines may be met, but the one or two missed ones may undermine the main deadline. For example, printing of letters, return forms, return envelopes, and other items for a promotional mailing may be completed, but if the address labels aren't ready, the mailing can't be carried out.

3. Mismanagement of employees.

One of the worst statements you can hear during the execution of your marketing program is one employee saying to another, "But I thought you were handling that."

You immediately know that some task hasn't been done. And if Murphy's Law is at work, the task that hasn't been completed is crucial to overall execution of the budget.

Such lapses occur because of ineffective management of people. It may be that the scheduling, the communication, or the follow-up were inadequate. But whatever the reason, an important task doesn't get done and the budget execution suffers.

Some specialized knowledge is required for each marketing implementation task. As I've noted, companies using direct mail must be aware of stringent postal regulations affecting envelope layout or risk having their mailings rejected. Users of telemarketing services should be prepared with detailed scripts that callers can use, or they risk having the service use an ineffective message. Companies advertising on television should be aware that by leaving a certain amount of their schedules flexible, they can qualify for reduced rates when television stations fill in last-minute gaps.

4. Ignorance about key requirements.

Because Syms has advertised on television for so long, it is well aware of the opportunities and pitfalls of television and radio outlets. At the top of its weekly television schedule (see Exhibit 10–1, page 254), the company mentions "opportunistic buys"—sporting events—that it plans in addition to its scheduled ads. In order to take advantage of those, however, it must get the material to the stations on time.

10

Timetables and Management

Executing the Budget: Smoothing the Process

Dealing with technical and timing problems is a planning challenge, and the secret to handling them is to anticipate them. Here are some suggestions for making sure that happens:

• Identify all the tasks that need doing.

For each budget item, make a list of everything that must be accomplished. For a newspaper ad, you need to allow for the brainstorming, copywriting and design, revising the copywriter's efforts, printing proofs, proofreading the proofs, entering the changes, and so forth. No matter what the marketing activity, you will invariably find that there are more steps required than you realized.

• Develop a schedule.

With the tasks identified, next develop a schedule. This can be done in a number of forms, depending on your personal preference and experience. Some executives like flow charts, others calendars. A growing number of project scheduling programs are available to run on computers.

Wall Street Games' version of a schedule is a cash-flow summary for its Collegiate Investment Challenge (see Exhibit 10–2, page 255). This technique is useful as it correlates the tasks with time and costs. The message is clear: If everything goes according to schedule, costs will be on schedule. (Potential variations are noted in the last column.)

Whenever possible, allow for more time than you think particular tasks may take. For example, if you are dealing with such outside contractors as copywriters and printers, allow for the fact that your revisions may not be tended to immediately.

• Schedule in extra time.

Once you have the schedule, make sure that someone has responsibility for making sure it gets done. By assigning tasks, you avoid dangerous oversights and build in responsibility. One example of how assignments can be made is shown in the Wall Street Games "Materials List" that is part of its budget (see Exhibit 10–2, page 255).

• Assign people to each task.

Once you have a schedule and people assigned to carry it out, set deadlines for each task. In my experience, deadlines tend to be met according to how much leeway people feel they have with them. Though you allow for extra time in your scheduling, there can be no compromising on the deadlines you establish. This message must be conveyed to everyone involved in implementing the marketing budget—employees and outside contractors alike. Failure to meet deadlines for anything except emergencies, such as serious illness, is cause for dismissal or loss of business.

• Establish deadlines, and strictly enforce them.

Beyond focusing everyone on the importance of deadlines, you should provide incentives to your employees for implementing the marketing budget according to plan. An approach used by Wall Street Games is that everyone in the

• Provide rewards for success.

10

Timetables and Management

marketing group receives a bonus on top of their base salaries depending on each marketing program's actual financial contribution. Of course, the program can only make its contribution if the budget is implemented according to plan. Your own incentive approach can be geared toward overall performance or tailored toward specific aspects of the plan; for example, if deadlines have been a problem in the past, there may be bonuses paid for implementing the budget on schedule, regardless of the results achieved.

• Find deficiencies, and correct them.

Sometimes, companies discover that obstacles to meeting deadlines and budget projections are the result of more complex problems than employees' failure to meet deadlines or poor communications. For instance, Wall Street Games discovered that outside advertising and PR firms were consistently unable to provide the quality and timeliness of service that Tim DeMello desired. He concluded that the amount of business he offered wasn't large enough to command the necessary attention at the firms. Because advertising and PR are essential to the company's success, he decided he had to bring them in-house.

The challenge in implementing your budget is making sure your marketing plan gets a chance to prove itself. By getting your advertising copy in too late to be published in a magazine or sending your product out after you promised it to distributors, you render useless all your research and analysis. The results you achieve won't be a true measure of the plan's accuracy and feasibility.

Monitoring Performance: The Key to Future Success

The marketing story doesn't just end with smooth execution of your budget. You need to know what went right or wrong in your plan execution and results.

In the last chapter, I discussed results in terms of marketing productivity. That is, you want to be able to correlate your marketing activities as closely as possible to sales results.

Here I am referring to a more detailed and trend-oriented approach to monitoring performance. Among matters that should be assessed are:

After the plan has been implemented, compare what was spent to your budget. You need to know how realistic your projections were so your next plan is more accurate.

• Spending versus budget.

Your should determine the number of prospects generated and where they came from. You want to know whether prospects came in via word of mouth, advertising, direct mail, or some other source.

• Prospects generated.

For retailers, determining such numbers with any degree of certainty is difficult, unless prospects use discount coupons or request a sale item that was announced in only one advertisement. When the source of the response can be traced, though, systems should be established for employees to monitor the numbers.

Syms, for example, intentionally delays advertising a new store for the first week it's open so it can determine

10

Timetables and Management

whether shoppers just happened to see the store or heard about it through word of mouth. The company also gets a base number to compare traffic and sales once its advertising program starts.

And once its television and radio commercials begin, the company urges its managers to listen closely for reactions from people who come into stores, says David Bernard, director of advertising. "We get surprisingly quick response to our ads," he says. "People coming into the stores say they liked the latest ads or they didn't like them. Because Sy Syms has been doing the ads for so long, people feel close to him and tell us what they think. We experimented with some ads in newspapers and city magazines not long ago, and we heard almost nothing about these ads. For us to hear nothing tells us that either we did it badly or we didn't pique their interest."

• Prospects converted.

You want to know how many prospects who respond to your ads or direct-mail campaigns are turned into customers. Ideally, you want to know how many from each marketing effort were converted, so you can assess its overall effectiveness. It's possible to generate interest in products or services and wind up with few buyers. When you know how many prospects were converted, you are obtaining data relating to marketing productivity, discussed in the last chapter, that is a key part of fine-tuning future marketing plans.

Of those prospects who turn into customers, how valuable did the customers become? Companies in different industries assess customer value differently. In businesses that sell onetime items, such as stores in tourist areas, the amount a customer spent may be the determinant. In businesses that value long-term relationships with customers, such as accounting firms, the measurement may be annual revenues generated per customer. Once again, correlate the quality of your customers to the marketing effort that drew the customers.

• Customer desirability.

When Things Don't Go According to Schedule

In certain situations—most commonly in start-up companies and with new products—marketing plans and budgets have a way of being so far off target as to render projections useless. Most typically, sales are either much slower or much greater than expected.

Take the case of the Power Jump Plus device that revitalizes dead car batteries without jumper cables. Jim Irons of New Bedford, Mass., a Vietnam War veteran and an electronics engineer, thought of it back in 1982 while out on a date. The battery in his date's car died, and neither Irons's car nor his friend's car had any jumper cables. "I figured there has to be a way to store power" to revive dead batteries, he recalls.

So committed did Irons become to developing such a device that he spent the next 12 years and $117,000 of his own money developing, patenting, and bringing to market the Power Jump Plus. His marketing projections were so

247

consistently optimistic that he wound up losing his apartment and car and becoming homeless, sleeping on a concrete floor in a building in which he worked to perfect his device.

There were encouraging developments along the way—approval from an American Automobile Association test, a patent approval, and sales to local public works and police departments—but sales volume wasn't enough to pay all Irons's expenses. Suddenly, by early 1994, his line of chargers showed signs of taking off. After selling 3,000 units for revenues of $200,000 in 1993, his company, Iron Chargers Inc., expected 1994 sales of 100,000 units, leading to revenues in excess of $3 million.

Talk about feast or famine. Not surprisingly, the notion of doing a realistic marketing budget seemed very unrealistic to Irons.

While Irons's experience succeeding with Power Jump Plus is extreme, it isn't unusual in terms of the frustration and dead ends that get in the way of seemingly great ideas and inventions. Such disappointments tend to occur when entrepreneurs are ahead of their markets. Technologists often see a tremendous market, but the market usually takes longer to materialize than expected.

The same phenomenon extends to nontechnology areas as well. For many unusual and innovative products, there will be flat growth for a long time before information percolates through the marketplace and the products take off.

Similar situations—though not as extreme as the battery recharging company—have occurred with such well-known products as Vermont Teddy Bear, Boston Chicken, and Mrs. Fields Cookies. The owners didn't just open for business to long lines of customers and rapid growth.

John Sortino began selling handmade teddy bears from a pushcart in downtown Burlington, Vt., back in 1981. Sales grew gradually—way below anticipation—over the next eight years as the company experimented selling through department stores and its own outlets. In 1990, with sales still below expectations, Sortino decided to try a different approach—The Bear-Gram. The company advertised its teddy bears in New York City as easy-to-send gifts available by calling an 800 number.

Barbara Haase, the company's director of sales and marketing, recalls that company officials expected "people to call up a little bit. It was off the wall, totally off the wall, and from then on we've been doubling our sales every year."

Late in 1993, Vermont Teddy Bear Co. went public and on its first day of trading, the stock rose from $10 to nearly $17 a share. Sales for 1994 were running at an annual rate of more than $17 million.

Similarly, Boston Chicken, a restaurant chain specializing in rotisserie-style chicken, existed as a single store in Newton, Mass., for several years after starting up in 1985. Even when it began adding stores in the Boston area in 1989 and 1990, expansion was slow. But in 1992, things began to take off and, by early 1994, the company had more than 200 outlets in 19 states, with annual sales estimated at $44 million. It raised $38 million in late 1993 via a public offering in which the stock was offered at $20 a share and climbed to more than $40 a share by the end of its first day of trading.

Of course, not all hot products require a long gestation period to succeed. Tomima Edmark, a Dallas entrepreneur, came up with the idea for TopsyTails, a plastic hair-styling device, while working as a saleswoman for IBM. In 1991, Edmark began filling mail orders from her home at night after work. A mention in *Glamour* Magazine and an appearance on QVC cable-shopping network had TopsyTails off and running. By 1994, the annual rate had reached $80 million, and Edmark was still running the business from her home. According to Edmark, "This isn't brain surgery. This is a good idea and I marketed it the best way I could."

10

Timetables and Management

Similarly, Barney the dinosaur burst on the scene. Sheryl Leach, a former elementary school teacher, produced home videos for sale at her father-in-law's video retail business and came up with Barney to entertain her two-year-old son back in 1988. One of the videos happened to land in the hands of a producer from Connecticut Public Television, whose own preschool daughter fell in love with Barney. The show "Barney and Friends" went on the air in April 1992 and, by the end of 1993, more than 200 Barney-related products were on the market; one publication estimated their annual revenues are as much as $500 million.

The key forces.

How is it that some products suddenly become so hot? No one knows for sure, but entrepreneurs, inventors, and business experts offer two reasons as key:

1. Persistence in the face of rejection. Clearly, entrepreneurs and inventors must have a strong belief in themselves and their products, even in the face of skepticism and outright rejection. Debbi Fields, founder of Mrs. Fields Cookies, recalls the brick wall she ran into back in 1977 when she sought a bank loan. She overcame that rejection by inundating one banker who seemed most interested in her venture with free cookies and she overcame market resistance by giving away cookies outside her first store. "Everyone said I would fail," she recalls. "I refused to take no for an answer."

Indeed, professional inventors see skepticism as a positive sign. One inventor who was trying to develop a new type of watering tool for gardens and greenhouses visited a plumbing supply store as part of his research to inquire about existing tools. "There were about ten plumbers there, and they said what I was proposing couldn't be done. Of course, that's what I wanted to hear."

2. An understanding of customer tastes and desires. The most successful products seem to be based on an accurate reading of consumers' preferences. Vermont Teddy Bear Co. took off when it plugged into consumer desires for "comforting, nostalgic presents that, unlike flowers and candy, are permanent and personal," observed a toy retailing executive. Tomima Edmark got her inspiration from a woman's French twist that caught her eye while she was visiting her mother in Seattle. And Sheryl Leach was focused on entertaining her two-year-old child when she made her Barney video.

Determining exactly what the market wants—and coming up with the package to satisfy its desires—is sometimes easier said than done. Jim Irons struggled for years to produce the Power Jump Plus at prices attractive enough to interest a mass market. He judged the price to be in the $40 to $90 range. It took Vermont Teddy Bear Co. eight years to come to the realization that convenience was as important as nostalgia in selling its product.

10

Timetables and Management

The Real Message

Successes such as Vermont Teddy Bear, Boston Chicken, and Mrs. Fields Cookies are really testimony to the power of the marketplace. Anyone can bake a cookie. Anyone can figure out how to make a teddy bear. And anyone can figure out how to roast a chicken.

Those companies that tune in to market needs and satisfy those needs are the ones that shift from underperforming their budgets to exceeding their budgets.

▶ Exercises

1. Make a list of all the tasks that need to be accomplished to carry out your marketing budget.

2. Assign deadlines to each task.

3. Formulate a schedule based on the tasks and deadlines.

4. Assign responsibility for each task to the appropriate employees or outside contractors.

5. Identify at least one reward you can use to motivate your marketing team to execute the budget as planned.

6. If you previously implemented a marketing budget, identify at least two lessons you learned from that effort that you are applying to your current plan.

7. Identify at least three criteria you will monitor to measure your marketing plan's effectiveness for use in writing your next plan.

10

Timetables and
Management

(Worksheets for this chapter are provided on page 300)

EXHIBIT 10–1

DALLAS TELEVISION

This is SYMS' basic television commercial schedule. The schedule will be supplemented by adding various sporting events. These are not listed because they are generally opportunistic buys.

Approximately one week prior to flight date you will be notified what has been bought, when it will air and what commercial copy will run.

WFAA	Channel 8	ABC	
Monday–Friday	5:30A–6:30A	This Morning Business	2 times
Monday–Friday	6:30A	Metro Traffic (sponsorship)	2 times
Monday–Friday	7:00A–9:00A	Good Morning America	2 times
Monday–Friday	4:00P–5:00P	Oprah Winfrey Show	2 times
Monday–Friday	6:00P–6:30P	News at 6	2 times
Monday–Friday	11:30P	Late Night	5 times
Monday		News after Football	1 time

KDFW	Channel 4	CBS	
Monday–Friday	6:00A–7:00A	News Sunrise	3 times
Monday–Friday	7:00A–9:00A	CBS This Morning	3 times
Monday–Friday	6:00P–6:30P	Channel 4 News	2 times
Monday–Friday	6:30P–7:00P	Hard Copy	2 times
Monday–Friday	11:00P–12:00M	CBS Late Night	3 times
Saturday/Sunday	Golf (finals)	Doral Ryder Open	1 time ea.
		The Masters	
		Bell South Atlanta Classic	
		Buick Classic	
		PGA Championship	
		NEC World Series	

KXAS	Channel 5	NBC	
Monday–Friday	6:00A–7:00A	Texas News	3 times
Monday–Friday	7:00A–9:00A	Today Show	3 times
Monday–Friday	6:00P–6:30P	News 5 Report	3 times

FROM THE MARKETING PLAN OF ★WALL STREET GAMES★

— EXHIBIT 10-2 —

COLLEGIATE INVESTMENT CHALLENGE:
EXCERPTS FROM THE BUDGET/SCHEDULE SUMMARY

— MATERIALS LIST —

PRODUCT CODES	PACKAGE	QUANTITY	USED INVENTORY	TOTAL	UNIT COST	EST TOTAL COST	VENDOR	DATE ORDER	DATE DUE	RESPONSIBILITY
CIC 51-01	Folder	17,500		17,500	$0.70	$12,250	Allied			Wilgus
CIC 51-02	Instruction Book	17,500		17,500	$0.27	$4,725	Allied			Lynne, Allied
CIC 51-03	Stock Guide	17,500		17,500	$0.40	$7,000	Allied			Jeff, Allied
	Registration Form	17,500		17,500	$0.30	$5,250	Allied			Scott, Allied
	Transaction Ledger	17,500		17,500	$0.12	$2,100	Allied			Scott, Allied
	Statement Envel. 9 x 12	70,000		70,000	$0.10	$7,000	Allied			Wilgus, Allied
CIC 51-04	Package Pouch	17,500	17,500	0	$0.03	$0				Trish
	Package Colation	17,500		17,500	$0.18	$3,150				Trish
CIC 51-05	10 x 13 Envelope	17,500		17,500	$0.20	$3,500	Allied			Allied
CIC 51-06	Perf Letthd	17,500		17,500	$0.04	$700	Allied			Allied

— CASH FLOW SUMMARY —

PRODUCT CODES	VENDOR	MATERIALS	EST. TOTAL COST	DATE ORDER	6/7 6/21 7/5 7/19 8/2 8/16 8/30 9/13 9/27 / 10/11 10/25 11/08 11/22 12/06 12/20	ACT. TOTAL COST	VARIANCE
CIC 51-01	Alllied	Folder	$12,250	8/30	$12,250	$12,250	$0
CIC 51-02	Allied	Instruction Book	$4,725	8/30	$4,725	$4,725	$0
CIC 51-03	Allied	Stock Guide	$7,000	8/30	$7,000	$7,000	$0
	Allied	Registration Form	$5,250	8/30	$5,250	$5,250	$0
	Cumputer	Transaction Ledger	$2,100	8/30	$2,100	$2,100	$0
	Allied	Statement Envel. 9 x12	$7,000	8/30	$7,000	$7,000	$0
CIC 51-04	Allied	Packing Pouch	$625	8/30	$1,350	$1,350	$825
	Allied	Package Colation	$3,150	8/30	$3,150	$3,150	$0
CIC 51-05	Allied	10 x 13 Envelope	$3,500	8/30	$3,500	$3,500	$0
CIC 51-06	Allied	Perf Letthd	$700	8/30	$700	$700	$0
			$46,200		$0 $47,025 $0	$47,025	$925

10

Timetables and Management

FINE-TUNING THE PLAN

Maximize Your Marketing Efforts

At this point, your marketing plan would seem to be complete. But in today's intensely competitive business environment, a marketing plan is never really complete. It needs to be regularly monitored, updated, and improved—ideally on a quarterly basis but at a minimum annually. Monitoring should go beyond measuring your plan's results and include refining your overall marketing efforts and developing new business opportunities. Your marketing plan should also be linked to your company's business plan to ensure that it is compatible with the manufacturing, sales, and finance areas.

This chapter looks at two aspects of the fine-tuning process: developing new opportunities and linking the marketing plan to other planning activities.

Exploiting New Opportunities

The marketing environment of the 1990s demands that executives tend to the basics of marketing strategy and implementation and come up with new, creative approaches to marketing. In your marketing plan, you may want to add a subsection within existing sections entitled "Future Opportunity Areas." Or you may want to lump these new opportunity areas into a section at the end of the plan. The actual method you use is less important than assessing and considering new opportunities. Among the areas most ripe for innovation are the following:

• Arranging partnerships. These agreements go under an assortment of names, such as strategic alliances, joint ventures, R&D contracts, licensing arrangements, cross-border partnerships, and outsourcing. Whatever the terminology, many companies have concluded they can't do everything themselves and can benefit from partnerships to compensate for weaknesses and build on strengths.

By the mid-1990s, thousands of partnerships were being arranged—more than 15,000 annually, according to some estimates. In many such arrangements, small growing companies with innovative products or services become partners with large corporations that have significant financial resources and established distribution outlets.

As one example, CareerTrack arranged to show its self-help and training videos on some American Airlines flights. CareerTrack gained exposure to high-powered executives and American obtained free entertainment.

11

Fine-tuning
the Plan

In other cases, the partnerships become major transactions in which large companies invest hundreds of thousands or millions of dollars in a smaller company's product development and marketing program. Not surprisingly, the most common such arrangements involve computer, telecommunications, biotechnology, and other technology companies, but increasingly, nontechnology companies are arranging partnerships as well.

The key to making partnerships work is careful evaluation of its goals by each partner. There must also be effective management of the partnership and open communication by the partners to anticipate potential problems.

In the context of market planning, partnerships should be explored to leverage limited resources and distribution outlets. However, executives of smaller companies should avoid the trap of looking to a partnership to somehow work a distribution or sales miracle that they have been unable to work themselves. Partnerships can supplement your marketing effort, not substitute for it.

• Working closer with customers.

There is a tendency by executives to concentrate more attention on attracting new customers than on satisfying existing ones. The need to satisfy existing customers, though, has become crucial.

Companies of all types are demanding closer cooperation with their vendors and suppliers. In many cases, large corporations have reduced the number of vendors and suppliers they purchase from, and insist that the remaining core group become increasingly responsive to the purchaser's needs.

From a marketing perspective, that means devoting substantial attention and energy to keep customers happy. Richard Worth of R.W. Frookies points out that one of his company's subcontractors that makes some of its cookies has obtained orders for Frookies from retailers the subcontractor deals with. Frookies reciprocates by promoting the supplier's products among certain Frookies customers. "It's an example of true cooperation," says Worth.

Few companies will be able to survive in the 1990s without having some sort of international, or global, orientation. That means selling and distributing products and services to customers in other countries or to foreign companies and travelers when they come to the United States.

• Exploiting international opportunities.

The Body Shop has been a master at operating in other countries. By 1990 the company reported that more of its revenues came from overseas markets than from its United Kingdom shops. In addition, founder Anita Roddick spends much of her time traveling the world in search of new product ideas and market information and data. "On a global scale, the potential is virtually limitless," she says. "The concept crosses national frontiers with ease."

Companies that want to be global must apply many of the strategy and implementation techniques described in this book to other countries. To be successful requires making adjustments to your strategy and implementation to fulfill the

11

Fine-tuning the Plan

needs of overseas markets. These needs will vary according to distribution, advertising, promotion, and other marketing approaches used in different countries. Conversely, executives can't simply assume that what works in the States can be easily repackaged for sale overseas. Sometimes, as in the case of The Body Shop, it can, but in other situations, cultural, language, and other differences become major obstacles to be addressed in the marketing plan.

• Using technology.

As noted, technology has become an ever more important part of the marketing equation. Companies must not only be prepared with databases of prospects, customers, and past customers to guide sales and promotion activities, but they must be able to access technology from different areas of the company for marketing purposes. Thus, marketing executives should have easy access to data on manufacturing lead times and accounts receivable, for example, to help guide market planning efforts. It can be counterproductive to undertake an intensive advertising campaign if manufacturing backlogs make it impossible to service new customers in a timely way.

• Developing new distribution outlets.

The old rules of distribution—that certain products are sold only via wholesalers or through manufacturers' reps—are being outmoded by the realities of the marketplace. Innovative companies constantly seek new ways to distribute their products. In some cases, companies bypass traditional distribution outlets, as when manufacturers avoid reps and sell directly to retailers. Thus, we increasingly see manufacturers establishing factory retail outlets in special malls or wholesalers going straight to consumers with their own direct-mail catalogs.

MicroFridge developed new distribution outlets when it took its microwave oven-refrigerator-freezer—a type of product traditionally sold through retailers—and sold it directly to colleges and hotels/motels. That way, it positioned itself exactly as it desired to the marketplace it wanted to reach.

It seems that everything in business needs to happen more quickly than it used to. Product development, manufacturing, promotion, and other activities all need to be completed faster. As part of their fine-tuning efforts, marketing executives need to measure how schedules are met—and constantly develop new ways to improve upon past performances.

• Reducing the expenditures.

Even when your company is performing well, you should never end the quest for ways to improve value to customers. That may mean, as in the case of CareerTrack, lowering your prices based on internal efficiency and productivity improvements. Or it can mean offering additional product or service features, with little or no increase in prices.

• Improving value.

The goal is to improve your offerings constantly in terms that customers can appreciate. Anita Roddick boasts that, "Unlike many major cosmetic houses, the percentage of base ingredients is high in all The Body Shop's products. For example, the Aloe Vera range has up to 98% pure gel

11

Fine-tuning
the Plan

from the aloe plant. Cocoa Butter Suntan Lotion contains 13% cocoa butter."

The idea is basic: Try to come up with ways to give the customer more than he or she expects.

Linking the Marketing Plan to the Business Plan

As key as it is to a company's success, a marketing plan becomes much more powerful when it is incorporated into a business plan. The marketing plan is then one chapter in a comprehensive plan that also deals with overall company strategy, products/services, and finances. Here are some ways to make that happen:

• Use the financial data.

The budget information developed for the marketing plan should be a key part of the cash-flow projections of your business plan. Because the marketing data is usually the most difficult to project, well-constructed marketing budgets can be invaluable in assembling on-target cash-flow projections. These, of course, support a business plan for a start-up and early-stage company.

• Integrate market planning with other planning.

Ideally, you should involve employees from other areas of the company as you develop your marketing plan. And the reverse should happen as these individuals develop plans for their areas. The purpose isn't merely to trade ideas, but to build on the knowledge that nonmarketing individuals bring to the marketing equation. Employees in manufacturing often have ideas for new features that can add value to a product. Those in finance may have approaches for lower advertising or telemarketing costs. All may be able to provide input for how better to exchange essential data to help everyone plan more effectively.

The marketing plan can't succeed with the backing of just one group in a company. It needs company-wide support. As an extension of the previous point, then, you should seek not simply to involve others but have them support the plan. They should see to it that the plan works—by assuring that products are ready when promised and support services are available as needed.

• Get others in the company to "buy in" to the marketing plan.

If the rest of the company isn't on board, the marketing plan can easily be undermined or sabotaged. If the plan isn't viewed as "their" plan, resentments can develop that lead to delays in delivering products.

Looking Ahead:
New Strength

Your marketing plan gives you and your company strength to compete on today's tough business battlefield. Having gone through the planning process, you gain unique insights, ideas, and confidence. You know you are dealing with the most important strategic and implementation issues confronting any company.

11

Fine-tuning
the Plan

Of course, you can't be sure you have always dealt correctly with these issues. As I noted early in this book, marketing is more art than science, and none of us can ever expect to be perfect. But if your marketing plan enables you to become a more accomplished artist than your competitors are, it will have accomplished a great deal. Here's hoping that it does.

▶ Exercises

1. Identify two potential partnership opportunities and candidates that would enable your company to expand its marketing opportunities.

2. Describe at least two approaches for your company to work more closely with its customers.

3. Describe at least one approach for extending your company's marketing reach internationally over the next two years.

4. Describe at least two ways your company can use technology to maximize the effectiveness of your marketing plan.

5. Identify two potential new distribution outlets your company will explore using during the next three years.

6. Describe at least one approach to improve your product's or service's value to customers.

7. Develop an approach for effectively integrating your company's marketing plan into your business plan.

(Worksheets for this chapter are provided on page 304)

11

Fine-tuning the Plan

EXERCISES

▶ **Exercises**

1. **Are any marketing misconceptions at work in your company? If so, describe them and provide suggestions for overcoming them.**

   _____

   _____

   _____

   _____

   _____

   _____

   _____

   _____

   _____

   _____

   _____

   _____

   _____

   _____

   _____

   _____

   _____

2. **Describe at least one driving force in your market that is counterintuitive.**

   _____

   _____

   _____

   _____

   _____

   _____

   _____

3. **Describe at least one problem that your company solves for prospective customers.**

    _____

    _____

    _____

    _____

    _____

    _____

    _____

4. **Develop and describe at least two unconventional marketing approaches you should consider for your company's products or services.**

    A: _____

    _____

    _____

    _____

    _____

    B: _____

    _____

    _____

    _____

    _____

5. **List and describe at least two emotional forces at work that determine success in your market.**

    _____

    _____

    _____

    _____

    _____

    _____

6. **List and describe at least three seemingly minor implementation tasks, or details, that must be dealt with to succeed in your market.**

A: _____

_____

_____

_____

_____

_____

_____

_____

_____

B: _____

_____

_____

_____

_____

_____

_____

_____

C: _____

_____

_____

_____

_____

_____

_____

_____

▶ **Exercises**

1. **Assessing Your Marketing Personality**

    Here is a list of the key components of the marketing personality. Rate yourself on a scale of 1 to 5 (with 5 being the strongest) in each category. A score of 3 or lower in any one category suggests you need assistance in that category.

Category	Rating (1–5)
Vision	
Creativity	
Sense of timing	
Ability to spot key trends	
Penchant for details	
Ability to change	
A long-term viewpoint	
Passion	
Focus	
A technology and information orientation	

Exercises

2. Preparing a Marketing Overview

a. Write a "case" about your company and the evolution of its marketing approach.

b. Use this case to prepare a half-page to one-page marketing overview that describes your company's approach for achieving marketing success.

▶ **Exercises**

1. **Which of the three types of marketing plans do you feel is most appropriate for your company to prepare?**

    Type of Plan   Comments

    A: Start-up or early
    stage strategic plan

    B: Aggresive growth strategic
    implementation plan

    C: Mature-company
    implementation plan

2. **Do you need more than one plan and, if so, which products/services should they cover?**

3. Using the material you wrote in answer to the exercise questions in Chapters 1 and 2, and your answer to Question 1 on page 275, list the six most pressing marketing questions facing your company at its current stage of development.

A: _____

_____

_____

B: _____

_____

_____

C: _____

_____

_____

D: _____

_____

_____

E: _____

_____

_____

F: _____

_____

_____

4. From your answers to Questions 1 and 3, develop a tentative table of contents for your company's marketing plan.

_____

_____

_____

_____

_____

5. **Determine how you will go about writing the marketing plan. What is your schedule for completing the plan?**

Projected date of completion: _____

Steps/Phases of plan completion: _____

_____

_____

_____

_____

_____

_____

_____

_____

_____

_____

_____

_____

_____

_____

_____

_____

_____

_____

_____

_____

_____

_____

_____

▶ Exercises

1. Describe the overall financial direction of your industry over the last 10
    to 20 years.

    _____

    _____

    _____

    _____

    _____

    _____

    _____

    _____

    _____

    _____

    _____

2. Describe the three most important trends that have affected your
    industry over the last 10 to 20 years.

    A: _____

    _____

    _____

    B: _____

    _____

    _____

    C: _____

    _____

    _____

    _____

3.   **Which industry segment does your company operate in?**

_____

_____

_____

4.   **Describe briefly how you expect the following to affect your company:**

The economy

_____

_____

_____

Government policy

_____

_____

_____

Cultural and social values

_____

_____

_____

Lifestyle trends

_____

_____

_____

Geography

_____

_____

_____

Technological change

_____

_____

_____

5. Graphically chart the product life cycle of each of your company's products and services, as far as can be determined. Using what has happened until now, project the rest of the cycle.

_____

_____

_____

_____

_____

_____

_____

_____

_____

_____

_____

_____

_____

_____

_____

_____

_____

_____

_____

6. Describe at least three possible scenarios for your industry and explain how each would most likely affect your position in the marketplace.

A: _____

_____

_____

_____

B: _____

_____

_____

_____

_____

_____

C: _____

_____

_____

_____

_____

_____

7. **Identify at least one discontinuity affecting your industry and describe how it could affect your company.**

_____

_____

_____

_____

_____

_____

_____

_____

_____

_____

_____

_____

▶ Exercises

1. Describe in 25 words or less each of the four most important benefits
    your company's product or service provides. (Repeat the exercise for
    each of your company's additional products or services.)

    A: _____

    _____

    _____

    _____

    B: _____

    _____

    _____

    _____

    C: _____

    _____

    _____

    _____

    D: _____

    _____

    _____

    _____

2. Prioritize these benefits.

    _____

    _____

    _____

3. **Label each benefit according to whether it is an emotional or a financial benefit.**

Priority	Benefit	Emotional Benefit	Financial Benefit
#1:			
#2:			
#3:			
#4:			

4. **For each financial benefit, calculate the financial savings or gain to the customer. Can you determine a payback period for your product or service? What is it? If it is longer than you want, can you think of ways to shorten it?**

5. **Describe three ways in which you will provide for the ongoing collection of knowledge and information to ensure you make appropriate adjustments of your marketing strategy.**

    A: _____

    _____

    _____

    _____

    _____

    B: _____

    _____

    _____

    _____

    _____

    C: _____

    _____

    _____

    _____

    _____

6. **How will the collection process be systematized in your company?**

    _____

    _____

    _____

    _____

    _____

    _____

    _____

    _____

    _____

▶ Exercises

1. Are your company's sales a result of primary or derived demand?

    _____

    _____

2. If sales stem from derived demand, list at least three benefits your company's products and/or services offer to end-users.

    A: _____

    _____

    B: _____

    _____

    C: _____

    _____

3. How do you communicate the importance of those benefits to your immediate customers?

    A: _____

    _____

    B: _____

    _____

    C: _____

    _____

4. Describe your company's precise segment of the market.

    _____

    _____

    _____

    _____

    _____

5. Indicate your company's position in its segment.

    _____

    _____

    _____

    _____

    _____

6. Explain how price fits into your company's positioning approach.

    _____

    _____

    _____

    _____

    _____

    _____

    _____

7. Describe at least two approaches you have planned over the next year for monitoring customer/prospect attitudes.

    _____

    _____

    _____

    _____

    _____

    _____

    _____

    _____

    _____

    _____

▶ **Exercises**

1. **Identify your three most important direct, or segment, competitors.**

    A: _____

    B: _____

    C: _____

2. **Name your three most significant industry competitors.**

    A: _____

    B: _____

    C: _____

3. **Identify and describe at least two indirect competitors.**

    A: _____

    _____

    _____

    B: _____

    _____

    _____

4. **Imagine that a major direct competitor has significantly cut its prices. Describe two possible responses from you, neither of which entails cutting prices.**

    A: _____

    _____

    _____

    B: _____

    _____

    _____

5. **List the four most important "what if" questions regarding competitors' actions.**

   A: _____

   _____

   B: _____

   _____

   C: _____

   _____

   D: _____

   _____

6. **Describe four ways in which you regularly obtain information about competitors.**

   A: _____

   B: _____

   C: _____

   D: _____

7. **Name the two most important pieces of competitive information you don't have but would like to have.**

   A: _____

   B: _____

8. **Specify two potential (legal) approaches to obtain that information.**

   A: _____

   _____

   _____

   B: _____

   _____

   _____

9. **Describe at least two things competitors are doing that you admire and would consider applying in your company.**

A: _____

B: _____

0. **Develop a competitor matrix for your company.**

COMPETITOR MATRIX
(Fill in the blank columns with key measurement criteria)

Company	Founding Date	19__ Estimated Revenue						Est. # of Customers	Est. # of Employees

11. Identify your company's four most important competitive advantages.

A: _____

_____

_____

_____

_____

B: _____

_____

_____

C: _____

_____

_____

D: _____

_____

_____

_____

_____

▶ Exercises

1. **Describe within each of the following categories the two most important types or components of information essential for you to communicate to your marketplace:**

Benefits information
_____
_____
_____
_____
_____

Product / service information
_____
_____
_____
_____
_____

Sales information
_____
_____
_____
_____
_____

Prospect / customer information
_____
_____
_____
_____
_____

2. **What is your overall approach for using this information to communicate with your marketplace? What information will you emphasize and how will you communicate it?**

Overall approach: _____

_____

_____

_____

_____

_____

_____

_____

_____

_____

_____

_____

Emphasis of information: _____

_____

_____

_____

_____

_____

_____

_____

_____

_____

_____

_____

_____

3. Prioritize and discuss each of the key communication options you plan to use. Explain the pros and cons associated with each one and why you think the advantages outweigh the disadvantages.

_____

_____

_____

_____

_____

_____

_____

_____

_____

_____

_____

_____

_____

_____

_____

_____

_____

_____

_____

_____

_____

_____

_____

_____

_____

4. **List and discuss at least two unconventional approaches for communicating with your market. Describe advantages associated with each approach compared with conventional approaches.**

A: _____

_____

_____

_____

_____

_____

_____

_____

_____

_____

B: _____

_____

_____

_____

_____

_____

_____

_____

_____

_____

_____

_____

_____

5. Describe at least one approach to micromarketing that your company could take as part of fostering an ongoing relationship with customers and prospects.

▶ **Exercises**

Begin putting together a marketing budget for your company. Go through
the following exercises as needed:

1. List the people who will work on the marketing budget.

2. List the marketing information and communication priorities for each
   of your company's products/services for the next year to reach your
   target market and carry out your marketing strategy.

Product/Service	Information/Communication Priority

3. **Determine how much you are prepared to spend on marketing activities.**

_____

_____

_____

_____

_____

_____

_____

_____

4. **Calculate how much each of the activities listed in your priorities will cost to carry out.**

_____

_____

_____

5. **Estimate the revenues you can expect to obtain from each activity.**

Information/Communication activity	Est. cost	Est. revenues

6. **Estimate the marketing productivity associated with each activity.**

    _____

    _____

    _____

7. **Revise your allocation and cost estimates as necessary to achieve your goals.**

Information/Communication activity	Revenue goal	Revised cost

8. **Determine what approaches you will use to measure results from each activity.**

Information/Communication activity	Assessment Standard

9.   Establish a timetable for implementing your budget.

Project name: _____

Marketing Budget Timetable

Item	Month 1	Month 2	Month 3	Month 4	Month 5	Month 6	Month 7	Month 8	Month 9	Month 10	Month 11	Month 12	
TOTALS													

▶ **Exercises**

1. **Make a list of all the tasks that need to be accomplished to carry out your marketing budget.**

2. **Assign deadlines to each task.**

Task	Deadline

3. **Formulate a schedule based on the tasks and deadlines.**

Project name: _____

Marketing Schedule, by task

Task	Phase 1	Phase 2	Phase 3	Phase 4

4. **Assign responsibility for each task to the appropriate employees or outside contractors.**

Task	Responsible Party

5. **Identify at least one reward you can use to motivate your marketing team to execute the budget as planned.**

_____

_____

_____

6. If you previously implemented a marketing budget, identify at least two lessons you learned from that effort that you are applying to your current plan.

    A: _____

    _____

    _____

    _____

    B: _____

    _____

    _____

    _____

    _____

7. Identify at least three criteria you will monitor to measure your marketing plan's effectiveness for use in writing your next plan.

    A: _____

    _____

    _____

    B: _____

    _____

    _____

    C: _____

    _____

    _____

    _____

▶ Exercises

1. **Identify two potential partnership opportunities and candidates that would enable your company to expand its marketing opportunities.**

   A: _____

   _____

   _____

   B: _____

   _____

   _____

2. **Describe at least two approaches for your company to work more closely with its customers.**

   A: _____

   _____

   _____

   _____

   B: _____

   _____

   _____

   _____

3. **Describe at least one approach for extending your company's marketing reach internationally over the next two years.**

   _____

   _____

   _____

   _____

   _____

4. **Describe at least two ways your company can use technology to maximize the effectiveness of your marketing plan.**

A: _____

_____

_____

_____

_____

_____

B: _____

_____

_____

_____

_____

_____

5. **Identify two potential new distribution outlets your company will explore using during the next three years.**

A: _____

_____

_____

_____

B: _____

_____

_____

_____

6. Describe at least one approach to improve your product's or service's value to customers.

    _____

    _____

    _____

    _____

    _____

    _____

    _____

    _____

    _____

7. Develop an approach for effectively integrating your company's marketing plan into your business plan.

    _____

    _____

    _____

    _____

    _____

    _____

    _____

    _____

    _____

    _____

    _____

    _____

    _____

    _____

    _____

INDEX

Index

Index